ADVANCE PRAISE

"Paul's book is clear, readable and practical. As Paul says, 'values are only true values if they are lived and demonstrated in day-to-day life' – or, as I often say, 'your values only have value if they come at a cost.' Paul brings practical insight into helping businesses create a practical purpose underpinned by real values."

JOHN G. LEE
Managing Partner, FIT Remuneration Consultants

"Alive: Cultivating Living Organizations for Success in a Digital Age offers an insightful and refreshingly accessible perspective on how modern businesses can thrive by embracing adaptability and engaging the often overlooked and untapped energy in organizations. It blends practical advice with engaging examples, showcasing how leaders can build more resilient and innovative workplaces and teams. This book is an inspiring read for anyone looking to cultivate a purpose-driven, collaborative organizational culture that can adapt and prosper in the increasingly dynamic world in which they operate."

RICHARD DEAKIN
CEO, Stratospheric Platforms, and former CEO,
NATS (National Air Traffic Services)

"Just as artificial intelligence threatens to further dehumanize organizations, Alive: Cultivating Living Organizations for Success in a Digital Age is an urgent reminder that businesses thrive when they are built around motivated and engaged people. I love the analogy to a living organism – in an era of digital transformation it brings back into focus the need for humanity at the heart o

STEPHEN GRAHA
Executive Vice President and Gener

"Paul has an amazing ability to distil complex corporate ecosystems into clear, actionable concepts that act as a toolkit for executives. Alive: Cultivating Living Organizations for Success in a Digital Age is a must-read for business leaders, and anyone interested in driving better business outcomes by aligning planet, people and profit."

SIMON BETTY
Head of Europe, Northwest Healthcare REIT

"At a time of hugely increasing pressure on organizations to 'perform', this is a timely reminder that the traditional mechanistic view still pervades our current management thinking. Alive: Cultivating Living Organizations for Success in a Digital Age presents an optimistic and hopeful alternative – and how to implement it."

PHIL EVANS
Director General, EUMETSAT

"Alive: Cultivating Living Organizations for Success in a Digital Age is an inspiring, insightful read that challenges traditional corporate mindsets and reimagines organizations as dynamic, evolving entities. Paul draws from his extensive experience to argue convincingly that organizations should be viewed as living organisms – characterized by purpose, adaptability, and a commitment to nurturing human creativity. His powerful examples, from Nissan's revolutionary team structures to Buurtzorg's self-managed healthcare model, highlight the transformative potential of this mindset. Paul's practical insights make Alive *not only a manifesto for organizational change but also a roadmap for achieving sustainable growth in today's complex, rapidly evolving world. This book is a must-read for leaders, managers, and anyone committed to creating a work culture where people, not just processes, drive."*

ALEXANDRA BODE-TUNJI FCIPD APM
Chief People Officer, Change Grow Live

"In this book, Paul looks to turn the tables on those organizational cultures which have increasingly positioned people as costs to be minimized and customers as a means to an end. Future talent expects a less mechanistic, more purposeful and empathetic organizational model. To deliver this we will need to rethink established doctrine and redefine what we mean by organizational success."

PROFESSOR NICK KEMSLEY
Executive Fellow, Henley Business School

"Companies anchored in the industrial-age methods of work are either dying or already dead. Paul expertly explains why this is happening, combining theory with his own vast experience and the experiences of others who are leading the new era of companies that are very much alive in the digital age."

ALEX HIRST
co-author of the bestselling
Workstyle: A Revolution for Wellbeing, Productivity and Society

"The future of work requires us to break free from preconceived notions of how organizations are shaped and managed. Paul's insights spur us to think about organizations as living organisms, providing a fresh perspective and roadmap to create thriving, sustainable organizations. I highly recommend it to leaders and consultants alike."

MARY CIANNI PHD
Clinical Associate Professor of Organizational Consulting,
New York University

"It is leaders who set the culture of an organization through how they behave. In my experience, the most successful organizations have a culture that empowers and enables teams to operate and evolve in support of a clear outcome. Alive: Cultivating Living Organizations for Success in a Digital Age *is compelling on how these more 'organic' organizations will be successful and enduring in the dynamic environment we all operate in today. But it also gave me invaluable insights into how to make change."*

LIEUTENANT GENERAL PAUL JAQUES CB CBE
Master General, Royal Electrical and Mechanical Engineers,
and former Chief of Army Defence Equipment and Service

"Most of us spend our entire life working for organizations we don't like, with people we don't respect, seeking outcomes that don't resonate with who we are. Alive: Cultivating Living Organizations for Success in a Digital Age *provides the inspiration, examples and guidance to bring people back to the centre of business, infusing soul into organizations and liberating human beings, within and around them, to support their evolution and success with autonomy, ingenuity and passion. A must-read to equip your organization for a brighter future."*

EMANUELE QUINTARELLI
Equity Partner and 3EO Micro-enterprise Leader, Boundaryless.io

"Leaning on his extensive experience helping drive organizational change, Paul challenges us all to think differently at a time when every organization needs to adapt to survive in a rapidly changing world. A living organization can break free from bureaucracy, command and control, and group think to rethink its purpose in shaping its future and the future for all of its stakeholders."

PETER CHEESE
President, Chartered Institute of Personnel and Development,
and Former Global Managing Partner – Talent and Organization
Performance Consulting Practice, Accenture

"The bible for the life-centred economy."

STEVEN D'SOUZA
Senior Partner, Korn Ferry, and award-winning five-time author and four-time TED speaker

"Paul provides salient insights into how a change in perspective can help reshape and recharge an organization's achievements. In exploring the analogy of a 'living organism,' he provides relevant examples of how this shift can influence the way people think and behave. It's a fascinating read and positioned to be a helpful tool in today's turbulent and competitive world."

JANET WINDEATT
former Head of Learning, British Airways

"During my 30-year career leading teams and organizations delivering complex engineering systems, I have often spent more time battling to adjust and enable traditional organizations than focusing on the technical integration challenges. So this book is long overdue and will help leaders to understand what is now important when organizing their teams and individuals for work in the 21st century. Paul's extensive experience and insights, combined with his practical, application-based approach, will help in challenging the ingrained habits and default understanding of how we should best organize people for work."

COLIN BROWN
former Technical Director, Crossrail, and Managing Director, CAPBROWN Consulting

"Only those organizations that can adapt at pace will survive the rapid evolution of digital change. Paul brings a unique view of how businesses that operate like living organisms are most likely to succeed in our fast changing world."

NICK ELLIOTT CB MBE
CEO, AWE

Published by
LID Publishing
An imprint of LID Business Media Ltd.
LABS House, 15–19 Bloomsbury Way,
London, WC1A 2TH, UK

info@lidpublishing.com
www.lidpublishing.com

A member of:

businesspublishersroundtable.com

All rights reserved. Without limiting the rights under copyright reserved, no part of this publication may be reproduced, stored or introduced into a retrieval system, or transmitted, in any form or by any means (electronic, mechanical, photocopying, recording or otherwise) without the prior written permission of both the copyright owners and the publisher of this book.

© Paul Lambert, 2025
© LID Business Media Limited, 2025

ISBN: 978-1-917391-12-2
ISBN: 978-1-917391-13-9 (ebook)

ALIVE

Cultivating living organizations
for success in a digital age

PAUL LAMBERT

MADRID | MEXICO CITY | LONDON
BUENOS AIRES | BOGOTA | SHANGHAI

WHY I WROTE THIS BOOK

"This place is like a gawky teenager – full of potential but lacking purpose and direction," said my boss at the global professional services firm that he and I had worked at for years. The frustration was palpable in both of us. We had many brilliant, fun and curious colleagues who had helped clients deliver everything from a brand-new mobile payments system across Africa to the Digital Railway Transformation of the UK rail system. Yet we could not get a couple of thousand pounds to make a video to show other clients what we had achieved and could do for them, because of the complex and inadequate internal processes in our own firm.

"We're about 20 years behind the rest of the industry and on the brink of extinction." So opened my discussion with the leadership team at a 7,000-strong engineering firm. Around various parts of their manufacturing plants, they were experimenting with 3D visualization of innovative designs using virtual reality and using the most advanced materials in the world. Yet their production processes were stuck in the Dark Ages and most people in the firm lacked the skills to use this technology. Bright-eyed and keen graduates had joined on the expectation of creating the future but felt stuck in the past.

"We're busy building shops when people want exciting destinations with entertainment, restaurants, offices, homes and creative spaces in our cities," said the director. This real estate firm could see the future but was busy still developing retail centres of the past. Why had they got stuck?

Why I wrote this book

Perhaps you share my mix of personal frustration and joy about the businesses, charities, government departments and organizations you work at?

Over a career spanning more than 25 years with small, boutique and global people – and organizational – consultancies, I have had the privilege of seeing people and organizations change and achieve amazing things. I have led work with a global child sponsorship charity with 700,000 sponsored children whose lives were being transformed because this amazing charity enabled ordinary people from the US and Europe to connect with communities and be part of their transformation. Together we shifted the charity from an old-fashioned letter-writing approach to building relationships between people of all ages through shared videos, stories, trips and project visits. I have also seen a change averse defence organization host immersive dramas involving over 7,000 people over 20 events to fundamentally shift their culture to do things differently. It convinces me that change is possible.

This is a time of opportunity, with significant shifts in the market and global context. We are seeing the reinvention of industries, with platform (ecosystem) businesses like Uber (which owns no cars) becoming the largest taxi firm in the world. Consumers and citizens are itching to buy goods from businesses that consider the 3Ps of planet, people and profit rather than just profit. Post-COVID, work has changed radically for many, with hybrid and technology-enabled work becoming the norm. Customers expect differentiated products like Nike's React Infinity Run shoes, which offer runners their own personalized colours and build of running shoes. Artificial intelligence is both automating lower-level professional roles and creating augmented human capabilities in areas like 3D design and filmmaking. Political and economic volatility, alongside scarcity of talent, is pushing for greater agility and creativity from people and organizations.

Ironically, this level of external disruption has been addressed with relatively conventional organizational responses. Most companies and corporations still adopt bureaucratic structures and mindsets to address the shifting needs of consumers. Accusations are rife that companies are keen to brand themselves as aligned with these causes – often referred to as 'woke' – without really responding to the heart of this change. Leadership is often 'command and control' in corporations, with people are seen as 'human resources' (units of economic output) and environmental changes amounting to 'greenwashing.' The issue is that *it's hard to change the outcomes without changing the system.*

My desire and passion are to offer an alternative to this stalemate through a fundamental shift in our mindsets. The premise of *Alive: Cultivating Living Organizations for Success in a Digital Age* is that *organizations, like people, need to be seen as living, evolving organisms, and that doing so results in fundamentally different ways of structuring and leading them.* Throughout this book, I have tried to use living analogies to show how much we can learn from ourselves and from our world about how to work and organize better – how to release the inherent creativity and uniqueness of humans. I've included a lot of practical examples and application exercises so you can begin applying these ideas to your own situation, even as you read. And I've tried to avoid the danger of 'inspiration without application' so I hope the examples and application exercises are useful to you.

It has been my privilege and pleasure over the past few years to be part of the debate and work around the future of organizations. I have worked on over 200 people and organization projects with clients from financial services to humanitarian relief, looking at how we release the potential of people. I've worked both in global technology consultancies like IBM and CGI and in business and people consultancies like Korn Ferry and PA Consulting Group. I've also worked in smaller consultancies, including the one I run today – Living Work Consulting. Around 10% of my time is spent running executive education for leaders at Henley Business School (which is in the top five business schools in the UK at the time of writing), debating and teaching on these topics. With fellow enthusiasts and practitioners, I have set up the EODF (European Organization Design Forum), which is the leading European practitioner forum for organization design professionals. Along the way, I have written for newspapers and journals and presented at conferences.

It is a fascinating time to be part of an organization revolution – to see brand new forms of networked and platform organization emerge. As you read, I hope the many stories in this book will be like postcards from the future and convince you that a new way is possible, and you can be part of it. Enjoy!

CONTENTS

Why I wrote this book   viii

SECTION A
Concept of a living organization   2–29

  CHAPTER 1
  The case for living organizations   4

  CHAPTER 2
  What is a living organization?   18

SECTION B
Bringing the living organization to life   30–215

  CHAPTER 3
  Starting with purpose   32

  CHAPTER 4
  Purpose is expressed through cognitive, physical and emotional attributes   48

  CHAPTER 5
  Uniqueness (differentiation and similarity) of capabilities   66

  CHAPTER 6
  Empower – to adapt and improve   92

  CHAPTER 7
  Coordination over hierarchy   114

CHAPTER 8
Continuous development and growth   140

CHAPTER 9
Growth stages in organizations   164

CHAPTER 10
Living in an ecosystem   176

CHAPTER 11
Releasing change in living organizations   196

SECTION C
Shaping and building living organizations   216–265

CHAPTER 12
Illness and health in living organizations   218

CHAPTER 13
Your journey to a living organization   246

Where now?   266

References   270

Acknowledgements   277

About the author   281

Book summary   283

SECTION A

CONCEPT OF A LIVING ORGANIZATION

CHAPTER 1

THE CASE FOR LIVING ORGANIZATIONS

AM I A MAN OR A MACHINE?

My first job. I watched the queue form at the back gate of the AP Products production works in Leamington Spa, UK, at 5pm, waiting for the security guard to unlock the gates to release the herd of workers itching to get home to their families. The plant produced key parts for cars that were popular in the British and European markets. It was clear that the workers didn't want to spend a minute more than they were contracted for on site. The aim was clear – do the hours, pick up the pay packet and repeat. Boredom was supplemented with a degree of resignation on their faces. After the first wave of workers left, others, mostly managers, departed in their cars in the half-hour following. There was a sense of 'us' (the workers) and 'them' (the managers) reflected in the clothes, conversations and luxury of the means of transport. In the factory, there were still remnants of this divide in reserved car spaces for senior managers and separate areas of the canteen for production ('blue-collar') and office ('white-collar') workers. The bureaucracy and separation of worker groups was not good for quality or innovation. Nearly 5% of all production had to be reworked and the plant was undercut by Asian factories with newer facilities and more flexible ways of designing and producing these parts.

That was over 30 years ago. The factory only lasted another ten years and was eventually demolished. The company had started in the 1920s, converting and maintaining ex-World War 1 vehicles for civilian use. The one millionth set of brakes was made as early as 1939 but this achievement was eclipsed when the ten millionth clutch was made in 1958.

In 1956 the company supplied an astonishing 50% of the brakes made in the UK and 85% of the clutches.[1] How did this glorious success story come to such a sad demise in 2005?

Transport yourself to a new scene, around 320 kilometres north outside Sunderland, where I worked a decade later. The Nissan car plant started production in 1987 with 1,100 workers. It produced two car models – the Almera and Micra – that became popular across the UK and European markets. With much of the UK motor industry in decline and a poor reflection of its heyday in the 1950s and 1960s, there was a degree of scepticism about the future. Yet five decades later, it was the most productive car plant in Europe, producing more than half a million cars a year and exporting to over 130 global markets. The plant had grown to support more than 6,700 jobs in 2018. It currently produces the Nissan Qashqai (petrol) and Nissan Leaf (electric model) – moving into the next era of road transportation. The plant supports a major tier one supply chain of over 30 companies and has recently invested £420 million into its battery plant and 100% electric Leaf model production at Sunderland.[2] As a result, North East England road vehicle exports have trebled, from just over £1.5 billion in 2000 to £4.8 billion in 2014, with one in every three cars made in the UK now being made in North East England.[3] Despite the challenges of the UK's exit from Europe (Brexit) and the shift to electric vehicles, the future still looks bright for the plant.

In my career, I have worked as a consultant on both these sites and seen the human, financial and physical reality up close and personal. My job has involved working with and interviewing many of the people in organizations like these. I have reflected at length on the human and economic cost of the failure to continue to innovate and engage people, and thereby produce quality products and services that people continue to buy. In my other (parallel) role as a business school lecturer on people and organizations, I've had a chance to reflect on these situations with reference to research and frameworks. This has led to interesting discussions and debates with the attendee executives about their own organizations. This mix of direct experience (from consulting) and reflection (in the business school) has led me to one simple but profound conclusion:

Organizations, just like people, are living beings that need to be nurtured and developed to be healthy and fruitful.

HOW DID WE GET HERE? A VICTORIAN LEGACY

There is much talk about the 'New Industrial Revolution,' often referred to as Industry 4.0.[4] However, if we want to understand how we think today then it's useful to reflect on the past. In historical terms, the first Industrial Revolution started around 1750 and lasted until around 1840. New machines were invented (sound familiar? Artificial intelligence?) that were combined with the flexibility of steam power. This led to huge factories being built in major towns. For instance, ceramics were produced in Staffordshire, shoes in Northampton and steel in Sheffield. Shipbuilding developed on Tyneside and Clydeside, and steel and chemical plants appeared along the Mersey and Tees. This resulted in people migrating to towns from the countryside. People were attracted to factory work by reliable pay. It was the birth of the modern world and Britain changed from a rural country with small industries to a highly industrialized and wealthy nation.

Initially, the small scale, diversity and flexibility of many Victorian businesses – characteristics that came from the craft groups that had come before them – were sources of strength. However, Victorian factories were often large and could employ over 500 people. The steam-powered machines became the centrepiece of these factories, with workers, often children, employed to operate them efficiently, often for hours. Life as a Victorian factory worker was hard and dangerous. The workers had to toil nonstop and could be fined or even sacked if they fell behind. Many workers were injured by dangerous machinery or became ill from breathing in fumes. Children were often the most vulnerable. Many worked as many as 14 hours a day and for this they were paid only a few pennies per week. The streets of Victorian towns would be filled with poorly dressed, tired-looking workers during the early morning and late evening.

However, as new technology was invented, so were new types of machines. Victorian factories became more efficient and made higher profits for their owners. The demand for goods increased as more people moved to towns, where they felt wealthier than in the countryside. Railways were built to transport all this material around the country quickly and cheaply. The rich became richer, and the poor remained very poor.

The factory and its organization were fundamentally viewed as a giant machine based on core assumptions:

- Machines and their products were both the essence and purpose of the factory.
- People were 'human resources' required to support efficient production and were expected to work for as long as possible and as quickly as possible.
- People (labour) was a cost that should be minimized; this led to children being employed for long hours in dangerous environments and being harshly disciplined. They were viewed as cogs in the wheels of production.

HOW MUCH HAS IT CHANGED?

The earlier examples were taken from my own experience of working in two different manufacturing environments during my career. The second example, from the Nissan car plant in Sunderland, was much more positive than the first, with AP Products. However, this progress is still far from the norm. Work across Western Europe and North America has seen an explosion of service industries over the past 50 years – from call centres to professional service offices – and observations of these show that the 'organization as a machine' approach is alive and well.

Take call centres. These offices look very much like post-industrial factories, with rows and rows of call handlers sitting at desks, in large offices, with their mandatory headsets typing at keyboards while they talk to customers. Typically, they are measured by how many calls an hour they can handle, often leaving clients frustrated with an incomplete resolution after a long wait. What does this feel like to the employees who are typically doing this as part of a long shift?

Call centres experience high turnover rates, with up to 40% of employees leaving annually, often due to stress and lack of support. According to one report, one agent said, "We're constantly under watch, with every second scrutinized, which makes it impossible to take a breath between calls."[5] A 2021 Talkdesk report highlighted that micromanagement and limited autonomy in handling calls were top frustrations. One employee shared: "The scripted responses make me feel like a robot, and any deviation leads to a reprimand."[6]

A way of viewing how well we are doing is reflected in the measure of employee engagement in work. The results are, sadly, consistently depressing. Gallup undertakes global surveys of many thousands of companies into the engagement of their workforces. In 2024, it found that only 23% of employees were engaged ("thriving at work") while 77% were either "quietly quitting" (not engaged) or "loudly quitting" (actively disengaged).[7] However, we know that employees who are actively engaged (believe in the firm they work for) and enabled (have the tools to make an outstanding contribution) are associated with radically better results, as illustrated in *Table 1*.[8]

ORGANIZATIONAL RESULTS	HIGH ENGAGEMENT	HIGH ENGAGEMENT AND ENABLEMENT
Employee performance Increase above expectations	10%	50%
Employee retention Reduction in turnover rate	−40%	−54%
Customer satisfaction rate	71%	89%
Financial success Revenue growth	× 2.5	× 4.5

TABLE 1
Relationship between engagement and enablement, and organizational outcomes

There's a sad reality and a great opportunity here. If we can crack the code of how to create organizations that are engaging and enabling to the humans that work in them, then we can unleash performance, keep great people, better satisfy clients and create financial strength. This book will draw out examples of where this is happening and offer you the keys to help you unleash the potential within the people you work alongside.

SO, WHAT DOES BETTER LOOK LIKE?

Buurtzorg describes itself as "a pioneering healthcare organization established in 2006 with a nurse-led, holistic model that has revolutionized community care in the Netherlands."[9] Its way of operating is human and patient-centred, and it avoids bureaucracy and, as a result, it has high client satisfaction rates. A 2012 study summed it up in the following way:

> Essentially, the program empowers nurses (rather than nursing assistants or cleaners) to deliver all the care that patient's [sic] need. And while this has meant higher costs per hour, the results have been fewer hours in total. Indeed, by changing the model of care, Buurtzorg has accomplished a 50 percent reduction in hours of care, improved quality of care and raised work satisfaction for employees.[10]

Buurtzorg itself says:

> Self-management, continuity, building trusting relationships, and building networks in the neighbourhood are all important and logical principles for the teams.[11]

As a result, from having just one team, Buurtzorg swiftly grew to have 850 teams employing over 10,000 nurses and assistants across the Netherlands, with 15 regional coaches supporting the teams as required.

During this time, it also grew in other areas of care, such as mental health, children and families, and also supported other Dutch international care organizations to adopt its model of care.

According to Buurtzorg's website, staff enjoy working for the organization and appreciate its self-managed structure, which encourages staff involvement. Buurtzorg won Best Employer of the Year in four out of the five years leading up to 2011. The organization says:

> [Our] back-office of 45 staff [keep] overheads low (8% as opposed to 25% in comparable organizations) taking care of payroll and invoicing to free up the rest of the organization to focus on care. Buurtzorg is now active in 24 countries and has a small international team to support its international work.[12]

So how does the model work and what is the thinking behind it? Buurtzorg's work is underpinned by its 'onion model' (see *Figure 1*). According to the organization, this model "starts from the client perspective and works outwards to assemble solutions that bring independence and improved quality of life."[13]

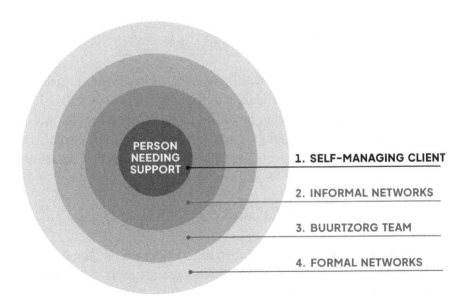

FIGURE 1
The Buurtzorg onion model

The onion model is focused on supporting people to be independent, with control over their lives and high-quality relationships with others. Each staff member "attunes to the client and their context, taking into account the living environment, the people around the client, a partner or relative at home, and on into the client's informal network: their friends, family, neighbours and clubs as well as professionals already known to the client in their formal network."[14] The choice and provision of support always involve the client and their informal network.

Buurtzorg aims to foster a spirit of entrepreneurship: "professional freedom with responsibility."[15] Responsibility is placed on all members of staff to develop the organization and its services. Each team of 12 staff concentrates on a single neighbourhood, and the organization describes its process as follows:

> A new team will find its own office in the neighbourhood, spend time introducing themselves to the local community and getting to know GPs and therapists and other professionals. The team decides how they organise the work, share responsibilities and make decisions, through word of mouth and referrals the team builds up a caseload.[16]

So where do we go from here?

Buurtzorg provides a wonderful illustration of the impact of unleashing the human spirit at work. Fundamentally, there has been a realization that an organization is a living organism made up of teams that need to be allowed to innovate and improve around a common purpose. I saw the same dynamics of the release of human potential that we see at Buurtzorg first-hand at the Nissan car plant. These included:

- **Clarity of purpose around outcomes** – such as 'healthy people' or 'quality, reliable cars.'
- **Cell/team-based working** – Buurtzorg's 12-person neighbourhood teams function similarly to Nissan's work groups, each of which deal with a stage of the production process.

- **Balanced multidisciplinary teams** – rather than having functions specialized around a single skill, each organization has well-balanced teams with the skills needed to tackle relevant challenges.
- **Ability to adapt in response to the needs of the environment** – this might be a patient with different care needs or the shift to electric, rather than petrol or diesel, cars.
- **Ability to balance work** – in each case there is still a need for some cross-cutting support (think Buurtzorg's back-office team and coordination software).
- **Growth and development** – unlike AP Products, which stuck to a rigid and conformist production process, there is an ability in both other companies to shape new teams and innovate around products over time.
- **Close links to external environment** – each is responsive to its customers/patients and each also chooses to partner with other agencies.

In the next chapter, we'll bring alive these dynamics of a living organization, showing how they parallel core biological principles that sustain life itself. We'll then start to unpack how you can bring these dynamics to your own workplace.

KEY LEARNING POINTS

- Organizations are shaped and managed with a mindset (which may be unconscious).

- Organizations that are shaped by a **machine mindset** will see people as units of production ('human capital') that are cogs in a machine designed to produce the ultimate product or service. They will be viewed as a cost to be minimized and made efficient, with little regard to their wellbeing and inherent value. People are secondary.

- Organizations that are shaped by a **living or human mindset** will see people as creative and value-adding parts of a human system that evolves to better serve clients and customers. There will be an expectation that people bring different skills and ways of thinking that will help the organization develop both itself and its offer over time. People are primary.

APPLICATION EXERCISE

Answer the following questions for your organization:

- Are most people engaged and interested in the work they undertake?

- Do they understand and believe in the purpose of the organization?

- Do people feel empowered to make a difference and improve things for your clients/customers?

- What image would people in your organization use to describe the way it operates? (Machine, person or living being, or another image?)

CHAPTER 2

WHAT IS A LIVING ORGANIZATION?

HAIER:
TAKING A SLEDGEHAMMER TO A MACHINE MINDSET

Today, the Chinese multinational company Haier Group is a major global seller of household appliances. But in the 1980s, it had a serious problem with quality. Many of the appliances were broken before they even left the factory, and customers were unhappy. When the new CEO, Zhang Ruimin, was put in charge of the "communist-era dinosaur," he discovered that workers were "sluggish, careless and so undisciplined that Zhang had to stop them from urinating on the factory floor."[17]

Zhang's way of addressing the problem was unique. As the company records:

> When a disgruntled customer returned a faulty fridge to the plant one day in 1985, Zhang inspected the factory's inventory and discovered that many of those were broken too. Frustrated, he lined up 76 flawed appliances on the shop floor and handed the workers sledgehammers. "Destroy them!" he commanded. Soon the factory floor was littered with fragments of plastic and metal. Zhang grabbed a sledgehammer – one of which is now displayed in the showroom – and smashed it into a fridge to make his message clear: workers must shatter their old ways.[18]

Haier has since gone from strength to strength, and in 2023 it reported revenue of over $35 billion. The sledgehammers have become legendary in Chinese culture, with one even featuring in China's National Museum.[19]

While the story is a powerful founding myth of the success of Haier, it is (like so many stories of culture change) about a more fundamental shift to a whole new way of thinking. In more recent years, Haier has captured this in its RenDanHeyi organizational model, which originated with Zhang. The RenDanHeyi concept has three elements:

- **Ren** – people with the spirit of entrepreneurship.
- **Dan** – value created for users.
- **Heyi** – alignment of people value creation and user value realization.

Its core principle is that the 'value of people comes first,' which aligns employee value creation with customer value.[20] Even before the idea was encapsulated in the RenDanHeyi model, Zhang was building a business around encouraging people to maximize their own potential (personal, financial) while creating value for customers and colleagues.

WHAT IS A LIVING ORGANIZATION?

Haier is a wonderful illustration of the transformation of a mechanistic, 'command-and-control' firm (under the Mao regime) to a people-centric organization that realizes the potential of individuals and teams as part of a business enterprise. Haier is built of cell-like structures called micro-enterprises, teams of around 12. Each team creates specific parts of a service or product and 'trades' (interacts) with other micro-enterprises to form the enterprise. Each team can innovate, agree people's roles and remuneration, and trade with other teams. We will look further at these ideas later in the chapter. However, it is clear that Haier perceives itself as a living organism where the teams (cells) interact with one another and the wider environment.

Biologists have identified seven key characteristics of living organisms that are fundamental to life. There has been life on earth for around 3.7 billion years, whereas the average life of a company in the S&P 500 is now 21 years (it was 32 years in 1965).[21] So, you are very likely to live longer than the company you currently work for. Life clearly has a lot to teach us.

WHAT IS LIFE?

Humans and other living organisms are fascinating and complex. The average person is estimated to contain roughly 30 trillion human cells. However, scientists have boiled the core characteristics of life down to seven core principles:

1. **Core purpose** – All organisms have core traits that define the design of their bodies and that they pass on to their offspring. Everyone's DNA is different, although a lot of the composition is shared through heredity (via our parents).

2. **Order of life (cells)** – Life is built of core structures called cells. Cells have a common basic structure.

3. **Specialization (of function)** – From the core structures of stem cells, we build up complex chemistry and capabilities through the specialization of these cells to release energy to perform different functions.

4. **Sensitivity** – Organisms adapt and respond to their environment. This might include everything from skin tone changing in the sun to developing the ability to walk.

5. **Homeostasis** – All organisms are able to maintain balance and stability. For instance, the human body normally maintains a constant

average temperature of around 37°C and varies by less than half a degree either side of this temperature.

6. **Growth/evolution** – Humans provide a wonderful illustration that organisms grow and develop over life. We spend around nine months incubating as foetuses in the womb and then move through well-defined life stages as infants, children, teenagers, young adults, mature adults and elderly people, before ultimately dying. At each stage, different cognitive, physical, emotional and spiritual capabilities develop.

7. **Reproduction** – All living organisms can reproduce and have offspring. They have a means for creating new organisms that share a high percentage of their DNA while introducing new variations.[22]

Out of these seven basic principles comes an astonishing variety of living organisms. These range from the microscopic bacteria that inhabit nearly every environment to those majestic blue whales that traverse the world's oceans. In the dense canopies of tropical rainforests, countless species of insects, birds and plants coexist in complex ecosystems, while the arid deserts are home to uniquely adapted reptiles and hardy vegetation that can withstand extremes of heat and scarce water supplies. Meanwhile, the deep-sea harbours enigmatic creatures, such as bioluminescent fish and colossal squid, which thrive in the crushing pressure and darkness of the ocean's depths.

Life is both simple and incredibly complex at the same time. I remember standing in awe in the Ngorongoro Crater, within a safari reserve in Tanzania, seeing the most extraordinary diversity of wildlife, including catching sight of all of the 'big five' (lion, leopard, rhinoceros, elephant and buffalo) within a relatively small area (around 250 square kilometres). It is hard to take in that this variety and beauty is based on seven basic life principles.

So why is it that so many organizations, full of humans who teem with creativity and life, can be so restrictive and short lived? Have we lost sight of the fact that organizations and teams, like people, are living human organisms?

LIVING HUMAN ORGANIZATIONS

The organizations that I've already described – Nissan, Buurtzorg and Haier – all show that something better is possible. At the heart of this idea is a belief that organizations reflect life. People and human potential are at the centre of this hope. Each of these examples shows how living organizations are based on a mindset and principles that parallel the seven principles of life. These 'living organization' principles are introduced in *Table 2*.

LIVING ORGANIZATION CHARACTERISTIC	BIOLOGICAL PRINCIPLE
1. Purpose driven Driven by unique purpose and identity	**Core purpose** DNA as basis of common traits
2. Cognitive/physical/emotional embodiment of core purpose In skills, structure and culture	**Order of life (cells)** Built of cell structures
3. Capability based Unique skills and culture	**Specialization** Complex chemistry/capabilities (built from cell structures)
4. Adaptation Changing over time	**Sensitivity** Adapt and respond to environment
5. Integration/balance Through cross-cutting mechanisms	**Homeostasis** Maintain balance and stability
6. Lifelong growth Growing and developing over life stages	**Growth/evolution** Grow and develop over time
7. Networked Linked across different units into wider alliances, networks and platforms	**Reproduction** Have offspring in a family network

TABLE 2
Relationship between the characteristics of living organizations and biological principles

Returning to our earlier examples, we can see reflections of these organizational characteristics in various ways. Buurtzorg has a strong **purpose (1)** built around creating "solutions that bring independence and improved quality of life."[23] This purpose goes beyond the patient's immediate need to look at the care support available through family and healthcare community (GPs, therapists) to sustain health. This purpose underpins the whole healthcare network and the **networked (7)** sources of healthcare support.

At the Nissan car plant, the different areas of the manufacturing plant are built around different teams. Firstly, there are three stages of production that cover body assembly, paint and final assembly. Each of the areas is then broken down into 'shops' staffed by teams that carry out specific tasks, such as the 'press shop,' which forms the external and internal panels of the cars. Teams are therefore **capability based (3)**, with mixed teams that include maintenance technicians, production workers, quality control and other trades that are able to complete a whole unit of work. Like the Haier teams, they own a whole unit of work and can plan, do and improve their own output.

Underpinning all these examples, it is noticeable that the firms put people and teams at the centre of work, recognizing that teams and organizations – like people – have a **core purpose embodied cognitively, physically and emotionally (2)**. Teams have overall capability (cognitive), structures and processes (physical), and a strong culture and shared mindset (emotional connection). At Nissan, there is a shared mindset and commitment to quality that runs through all the teams, even though they vary in their purposes, capabilities and outputs.

Each of the examples has different ways of **maintaining integration and balance (5)**. Haier has industry and shared service platforms that provide sector/market alignment (e.g. they focus on a particular market, such as the UK, or a product, such as dishwashers) and services (such as HR and finance support). At Nissan, this comes through a partnership model, with HR and finance functioning through business partners.

Fundamental to all the models is the **adaptive (4)** nature of the enterprise. Buurtzorg has a relatively simple model of growth and reproduces itself in a networked way. Where there is a community with a perceived need, a new team is formed. The team's first task is to establish a **network (7)** of relationships with patients and providers to understand the need. They then organize themselves and ensure they have the right skills to match the client's needs. They may create another team to cover a different area or demographic. The principle is of a growing cellular, self-organizing team structure that mirrors the environment it finds itself in over its life.

Haier is a larger network than Buurtzorg and has reached a stage where it is clear about the different stages of evolution – i.e. **lifelong growth (6)** – of the business. This provides a depth of strategy to its purpose so broad priorities are clear while individual teams can still manage themselves. Since its foundation in 1984, Haier has gone through five seven-year cycles, from establishing the brand (1984–1991) to diversification (1991–1998), internationalization (1998–2005), global branding (2005–2012), networking (2012–2019) and ecosystem building (2019–present). The interesting reflection is that this was not planned, in the traditional sense of a strategic plan, but resulted from grasping opportunities at each stage of development.[24] It is certainly a result that a strategic planning department would be pleased with, but it has come from the natural evolution of an adaptive business!

KEY LEARNING POINTS

Living organisms embody seven biological principles:
1. **Core purpose** – DNA as basis of common traits
2. **Order of life (cells)** – built of cell structures
3. **Specialization** – complex chemistry/capabilities (built from cell structures)
4. **Sensitivity** – adapt and respond to environment
5. **Homeostasis** – maintain balance and stability
6. **Growth/evolution** – grow and develop over time
7. **Reproduction** – have offspring in a family network

In the same way, living organizations are based on seven principles:
1. **Purpose driven** – driven by unique purpose
2. **Cognitive/physical/emotional embodiment of core purpose** – in skills, structure and culture
3. **Capability based** – unique skills and culture
4. **Adaptive** – changing over time
5. **Integration/balance** – through cross-cutting mechanisms
6. **Lifelong growth** – growing and developing over life stages
7. **Networked** – linked across different units into wider alliances, networks and platforms

APPLICATION EXERCISE

LIVING ORGANIZATION PRINCIPLE	Machine — Where You Sit — Living
Purpose driven Driven by unique purpose and identity	Focus on profit ←——→ Strongly articulated and owned purpose
Cognitive/physical/ emotional embodiment of core purpose In skills, structure and culture	Rigid/fixed/top down ←——→ Flexible/responsive
Capability based Unique skills and culture	Single-function units ←——→ Mixed-capability focused teams
Adaptive Changing over time	Defined and fixed ←——→ Evolving and adaptive
Integration/balance Through cross-cutting mechanisms)	Top-down bureaucratic ←——→ Multiple coordination mechanisms
Lifelong growth Growing and developing over life stages	Fixed team/unit role ←——→ Adapt over different stages of maturity
Networked Linked across different units into wider alliances, networks and platforms	Fixed system ←——→ Porous boundaries

SECTION B

BRINGING THE LIVING ORGANIZATION TO LIFE

CHAPTER 3

STARTING WITH PURPOSE

**Living Organization Characteristic 1:
Purpose Driven**

- A human's unique purpose is encoded in their DNA and being.
- An organization's purpose is underpinned by core values and ways of being.

ARGUING OVER THE FUTURE

It was a robust and lively discussion. I was running a workshop with the senior leaders of a rail engineering firm about how they planned to organize engineering and project management to deliver some major upcoming projects in the UK and Singapore. The firm had over a thousand engineers and several hundred project management staff but recognized that the rigid, siloed structures were not going to allow them to tackle these big programmes and share key staff. We had identified that there was a core of around 10-20 highly experienced systems engineers who were able to lead the integration of these programmes but were locked into functional structures where they and the company had lost sight of the big picture.

We started the discussion by talking about how we could design the organization to be more flexible and the principles behind this. However, the discussion turned into an argument between the CEO and the engineering director. At stake, they realized, was the purpose of the business. The CEO said the purpose was to be a "cash register" – we collect money from our customers, who need working railways, and pay our staff to deliver the railways, to deliver a profit to the shareholders. The engineering director said the purpose was to "provide great rail transport solutions." Who was right? Why was it important?

The CEO was clearly the person in charge and his mindset was reflected in the company structure. The various functions were seen as cost centres run to budgets, so managers held tightly to their best staff to deliver their remit. Success was seen as delivering the defined functional outputs to time and budget, with each function aiming to demonstrate individual success.

The engineering director had a different view. He saw that everyone needed to buy into a bigger, shared vision to be successful. He envisaged engineers and project managers working across a range of projects with a view to ensuring the right skills on the right projects at the right time to make them successful. This would rely on managers being ready to share their best people for the greater good and purpose of the organization and their clients. Making the best choices on priorities would rely on leaders sharing and releasing key people and resources if there was a greater need elsewhere.

The debate in the room raged further. One senior engineer spoke passionately about why he had entered the profession over 20 years before. He spoke about how his family's legacy with the railways dated right back to Isambard Kingdom Brunel and the first Great Western Railway line, from London to Bristol, back in 1841. The firm had deep roots in the history of the area (it was headquartered near Bristol) and many in the room nodded in agreement. They weren't in the business just to make money; they wanted to make modern railways that their parents would be proud of. They wanted to innovate and create great solutions that fit the upcoming digital age.

The good news is that the story had a happy ending. There was an agreement in the room that financial, organizational and customer success were all achieved when people bought into this higher purpose. Everyone needed a shared vision of providing "great rail transport solutions" because this would drive the innovation they needed to keep up in the industry (competitors were hot on their heels with new digital signalling and transport solutions) and deliver projects on time and to budget (by flexing resources to meet key priorities). The firm adopted new project-based structures to support this flexible working, based on the shared vision of delivering great transport solutions rather than just an in-year profit. It became the jewel in the crown of the wider engineering group and was eventually bought by the global market leader as the core of its European business.[25]

The conclusion of the debate was that an organization's purpose is vital. For the engineers, knowing they were part of something beyond themselves, in a shared endeavour, was as important for them as employees as it was for them as individuals. People without a sense of purpose become demotivated and depressed. In the same way, organizations without a clear purpose disengage their employees and drive down productivity.

THE STORY REPEATS:
ORGANIZATIONS NEED IDENTITY AND PURPOSE

I led two significant projects for a large shipyard owned by a UK defence company. The shipyard had been founded in 1871 and had then changed ownership over many years. In its home town, many families had two or even three generations that had worked at 'the shipyard.' My employer and I became engaged with the company in 2014 to support them to expand from around 3,000 to 7,000 people to build a new class of ships. However, we found division between management and workers and unrest vocalized through the trade unions. For long-term success, it was essential that the current workforce and management pulled together and created a great place to work. So, we engaged different workforce groups and leaders through interviews, focus groups and surveys.

A clear conclusion emerged about how to integrate and galvanize all staff towards a common goal. Everyone had pride in the product. When a new ship was launched, the whole town would stop and turn out to see the launch. It was an incredibly impressive and emotive moment when a military vessel worth several hundred million was launched for the first time and set out protect the UK's peace and future. Leaders, workers and families were united in common pride and these events were typically accompanied by a royal visit. We built on this pride through a new 'employee brand' focused on pride in the history, evolution and innovation of 'the yard' over more than a century. This helped to attract nearly 4,000 new workers and a hard-won agreement over new ways of working on the new ships.

This isn't just true of product companies – it's a pattern repeated in a multitude of highly successful companies. In order to galvanize employees and other stakeholders, the purpose needs to be meaningful to human progress while specific enough to show the connection to the work of today and tomorrow. *Table 3* provides examples of purpose statements for ten well-known companies. These purpose statements are clearly aspirational, and the test of a well-run company is the degree to which the employee and customer experience matches these statements.

COMPANY	PURPOSE STATEMENT
Google	To organize the world's information and make it universally accessible and useful.
Microsoft	To empower every person and every organization on the planet to achieve more.
Amazon	To be Earth's most customer-centric company, where customers can find and discover anything they want to buy online.
Apple	To make the best products on Earth, and to leave the world better than we found it.
Tesla	To accelerate the world's transition to sustainable energy.
Coca-Cola	To refresh the world in mind, body, and spirit, to inspire moments of optimism and happiness through our brands and actions.
Nike	To bring inspiration and innovation to every athlete in the world. If you have a body, you are an athlete.
Facebook (Meta)	To give people the power to build community and bring the world closer together.
Disney	To entertain, inform, and inspire people around the globe through the power of unparalleled storytelling.
Airbnb	To create a world where anyone can belong anywhere, providing healthy travel that is local, authentic, diverse, inclusive, and sustainable.

TABLE 3
Example company purpose statements[26]

LIVING ORGANIZATIONS HAVE A UNIQUE PURPOSE

These stories and examples illustrate our first living organization characteristic: living organizations have a unique purpose. While this statement may, at first, appear a little generic, the examples in *Table 3* demonstrate that purpose emerges from the work (products and services) developed by employees, particularly during the founding period of a company. Purpose is 'discovered' as the shared passion and motivation of employees comes together to create a valuable contribution to people's lives and society. Apple was founded on the premise of creating products that people could intuitively use, including the unique user interface and the mouse controller. Effective purpose statements can never be a top-down marketing motto but need to reflect why people are motivated and engaged in their work. Authenticity in organizations is as fundamental as it is for individuals.

So, what are the essential elements of the identity and purpose of an organization? Linked to the analogy of organizations as living organisms, purpose can be seen as the 'seed' that the organization grows from. Living organisms seek to be 'fruitful,' producing the structure and life that is held in the code of DNA. *Figure 2* shows the DNA from which an organization grows.

Chapter 3 — Starting with purpose

'SEED' = PURPOSE	**'POTENTIAL' = VISION/MISSION**
This is identified with three principal elements: • **Core purpose** – overriding reason for existence (see examples in *Table 3*) • **Core values** – essential and enduring 'ways of being,' which may be expressed as principles, values or tenets (e.g. 'making it happen') • **Core behaviours** – these are non-negotiable behaviours that describe *how* we embody the core values (e.g. delivering on our commitments)	The seed gives the organization a foundation, but the vision/mission gives the organization an expression of what it can become. The vision/mission may be expressed in a number of ways, such as: • Company long-term goals • Mission statement • Vision statement • Images of the future

FIGURE 2
Purpose is expressed in a purpose statement, values, behaviours and vision

THE VALUE OF PURPOSE IN ORGANIZATIONS

In their book *Built to Last*, Jim Collins and Jerry Porras report the findings of a six-year study of "visionary companies," which are characterized by having a strong, shared core purpose, shared values and a long-term vision. Over a period of 64 years, these companies outperformed the stock market by 15 times. They show that clarity of purpose, identity and values led to enduring financial performance in a way that a pure profit focus did not. Beyond the financial viewpoint, these companies were widely admired by other business leaders, had made an indelible impact on the world, and had also been through multiple generations of CEOs and products. In other words, they were successful long term. This detailed empirical study provides evidence that viewing an organization as a living organism rather than just a 'profit factory' is the key to both sustainability and long-term financial success.[27]

If underperformance due to lack of purpose is a concern, then a greater concern should be the overall survival rates of large companies. By 2018, the average lifespan of a US S&P 500 company had fallen by almost 80% over the previous 80 years (from 67 to 15 years), and 76% of UK FTSE 100 companies had disappeared over the previous 30 years.

In the 1980s, leaders at Shell, under the direction of Arie de Geus, studied corporate longevity in detail. In his book *The Living Company*, Arie identifies the characteristics of companies that achieve long-term sustainability across an evolving set of market offers and sustained profitability. These characteristics are fourfold: sensitivity to the world around them, awareness of their identity, tolerance of new ideas and conservatism in financing. We, again, see the centrality of purpose and identity to successful companies. Managers in these 'living companies' are chosen mostly from within and consider themselves to be stewards of a long-term enterprise.[28]

WHAT DOES PURPOSE LOOK LIKE IN PRACTICE? HOW DO WE 'MAKE IT REAL'?

While there is much research to demonstrate the power of purpose and identity, it is vital to 'make this real' to employees, customers, leaders, suppliers and partners. There are some core principles about purpose and values in organizations that need to be understood to deliver them in practice:

- **Purpose is discovered** – It is based on the reasons why the organization was founded and the enduring stories that people tell about why they work there. Interviews, focus groups and observation are the best means to uncover the purpose beneath the surface of organizational life.
- **Shared values underpin the purpose** – Beneath the purpose, there are core values that are non-negotiable to committed employees of the organization. They form the basis of culture and the company's employee value proposition to perspective employees.
- **Values need to be demonstrated in day-to-day behaviours** – Unless people see values demonstrated (particularly by leaders) consistently in day-to-day interactions, then the core purpose will wane, and the organization will weaken.
- **As organizations grow, it is important to make purpose, values and behaviours explicit** – Early on in the life of an organization, there are a few people with a lot of shared history, so purpose and values are intuitively grasped. As organizations grow to hundreds and thousands of people, it is important to collate and communicate purpose and values consistently.

So how can we capture, develop and communicate purpose and values? *Figure 3* provides a helpful framework that relates purpose, values and behaviours.

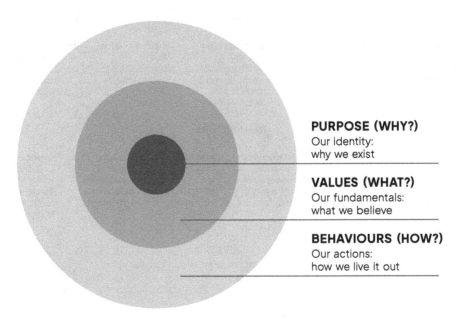

FIGURE 3
Purpose, values and behaviours framework

To aid understanding, *Figure 4* on the next page shows an example of this framework for a hypothetical real estate firm that creates iconic spaces for people to live, work and relax in.

ALIVE

PURPOSE
To create vibrant, sustainable destinations and spaces where people can live, work and enjoy themselves, delivering value for all stakeholders, including investors, tenants and communities.

VALUES				
Be bold – Embrace innovation, take smart risks and lead with confidence.	**Be responsible** – Commit to sustainability and responsible decision-making.	**Be enterprising** – Act with an entrepreneurial spirit, driving growth and opportunities.	**Be collaborative** – Foster partnerships and teamwork across the business.	**Be ethical** – Uphold integrity and act transparently in all dealings.

BEHAVIOURS					
Accountability – Take ownership of actions and outcomes.	**Innovation** – Seek new ways to improve and create value.	**Sustainability** – Integrate sustainability into every decision.	**Client focus** – Prioritize the needs of tenants, customers and partners.	**Inclusivity** – Create a diverse and welcoming environment.	**Teamwork** – Collaborate effectively across all levels and teams.

FIGURE 4
Purpose, values and behaviours in a real estate firm

There are a number of observations to be made about the elements of this framework:

- **Purpose is inspiring, broad, visionary and linked to human progress** – A purpose statement needs to motivate and excite those who read it, resonating with their experience of the organization. It should relate to a core human need (in this case it is about "creating vibrant, sustainable destinations and spaces where people can live, work and enjoy themselves" rather than just property) and focus on the betterment of humanity.
- **Values provide the 'what'** – Values should say what we do to bring the purpose to life and what customers and clients can expect from us. This is typically characterized by the (excellent) standards that we hold ourselves to, our attitude (e.g. enterprising, friendly), our respectful attitude (e.g. towards people and diversity) and our ongoing desire to improve ("Be bold").

- **Behaviours describe how we will act** – Values are only true values if they are lived and demonstrated in day-to-day life. Typically, each value is expressed through a number of behaviours, such as integrity, reliability and accountability, which are linked to a single value (e.g. "Be bold" links to "innovation" and "client focus").

Perhaps this is a good opportunity to reflect on why you work for the organization that you do and what drew you to the organization in the first place. Is there an intuitive match between what you stand for and what the organization is about? Did certain people demonstrate a way of being that attracted you? What did people communicate as important and central to the organization?

KEY LEARNING POINTS

- Living organizations focus on purpose first and profit second.

- Various research sources show that living organizations sustain success (financial and impact) over the long term.

- A strong purpose should be discovered – rather than created – based on the founding vision and the enduring stories of employees, partners and customers.

- A simple strapline and statement should be created to provide a motivating and explicit purpose for the endeavours of all parts of an organization (e.g. Tesla: "To accelerate the world's transition to sustainable energy").

- Values and behaviours flow from purpose – they are the 'what' and the 'how' of the purpose.

- Values reflect the enduring beliefs of the organization (e.g. "We hold ourselves to the highest standards").

- Behaviours reflect the specific ways in which these values are demonstrated in day-to-day work at all levels within the organization and in relationships with suppliers and customers (e.g. integrity, accountability, reliability).

APPLICATION EXERCISE

Consider the purpose, values and behaviour grid introduced in *Figure 4* in relation to your own organization. Have a go at populating a similar grid for yourself. Does the organization already have an explicit statement of purpose, behaviours and values? Do you see it demonstrated in practice? Is it a true reflection of the organization or does it need to be updated?

CHAPTER 4

PURPOSE IS EXPRESSED THROUGH COGNITIVE, PHYSICAL AND EMOTIONAL ATTRIBUTES

Living Organization Characteristic 2: Embodiment in Cognitive, Physical and Emotional Attributes

- Human purpose is expressed through our cognitive, physical and emotional faculties.
- Organizations and teams have cognitive (skills and capabilities), emotional (feelings) and physical (structure and processes) attributes.

CHANGE INVOLVES EVERYONE AND EVERYTHING

My team and I had been working with the Defence Engineering organization for over a year. As a team, we'd be helping them to ensure that their teams delivered safe and effective equipment to front-line personnel involved in vital overseas peacekeeping and military operations. However, a series of accidents over the past decade or so had proved that staff weren't all aligned in delivering this mission. They often felt it was a small number of safety engineers who were responsible for the mission, and jobs in other areas (like HR and finance) were seen as unconnected to this central goal. A major accident on an aircraft that led to several deaths, a fire on a maritime vessel and an explosion on a land vehicle had combined to send a strong message that things needed to change.

We had made a great start. We had looked at the end-to-end process of how equipment was manufactured, checked and signed off. We had examined the roles of those directly involved, the people and technology that they were supported by, and the skills required to deliver the mission successfully. We had looked at the governance process that resulted in signing off the equipment and whether the right people were involved. It was all positive but not enough. Out of the 7,000 people involved, there was a core of a few hundred (mainly engineers and some leaders) who saw this vital mission as part of their role.

What was missing? Fundamentally, all staff needed to be united around a central purpose and vision to "deliver safe-to-operate equipment to the front line." Yet this mindset wasn't grounded in 'hearts and minds' and owned across all 7,000 staff. What should we do?

We began to assemble the stories of past incidents and determine what had gone wrong in past accidents. We interviewed people who knew first-hand why things had gone wrong. Often, they said there was a lack of money to make changes (a finance problem), that people lacked skills (an HR problem) or that the right people hadn't been assembled as a team (a project management problem). However, the problem was organization-wide, not just an 'engineering problem.' In the process, we heard the passion of the people involved to ensure these incidents didn't happen again as they recounted lives devastated and deep personal loss.

Having collected the stories of these people, we contacted a specialist drama company that reenacted safety incidents. They had created a 1.5-hour drama based on the Piper Alpha oil rig disaster. This was a catastrophic oil-platform explosion and fire in the North Sea on 6 July 1988 that had resulted in the deaths of 167 workers and became the world's deadliest offshore oil disaster. The tragedy had been exacerbated by inadequate safety procedures and failed emergency response systems, and it led to significant changes in offshore oil and gas industry safety regulations.

The reenactments were 1.5-hour immersive dramatization of the stories of four major military accidents related to the work of the engineering organization. Each story was 15-minutes long, followed by time for the audience to ask questions, discuss where things had gone wrong and what the organization could do to avoid the disaster happening in the future. People from HR, finance, procurement, project management and many other functions saw that they were part of the problem and the solution. Minds were changed. The dramatization was performed to audiences of 400–600 people per show and delivered to a total of 7,000 people. A camera and production crew captured the dramas on film so segments could be used in future safety and organizational training.

There was an immediate impact on safety. Engagement across staff in safety decision-making shifted from below 50% to between 80% and 90%. We were flooded with support for the new initiative, and it led to a major communications campaign called Spotlight on Safety that was taken up by the British Army.

What was the key to this change? To take a metaphor from the human body, it shifted from head knowledge (cognitive understanding of purpose) to heart engagement (emotional link to purpose) and became part of the mindset and purpose of the organization, covering every person. This was the vital point of cultural shift. One of the directors said that it was the most successful change in the organization in the past decade because people owned and lived the outcomes.

THE ORGANIZATION AS A MACROCOSM OF THE INDIVIDUAL

The above story highlights how healthy organizations reflect many of the characteristics of healthy individuals. We may talk about a young person who hasn't yet "developed a sense of purpose" and is lacking direction in their life as a result. In the same way, we find organizations that "lack a common sense of purpose" and where people are consequently "pulling in different directions."

Therefore, we see that organizations and teams reflect the nature of individuals. *Figure 5* highlights four elements of an individual that are core to their nature and shows how they relate to organizations. At heart, people have a **purpose** that is unique to them. For example, we might say someone is a natural coach who has strong values around the importance of people and their potential. They then bring a set of communication skills and psychological understanding that is part of their **cognitive** make-up, and this enables them to develop others effectively. The person typically brings **physical** characteristics that enable them to coach and develop others. If this is sports coaching, this might include physical fitness. In a teaching context, this might be expressed through engaging ways of communicating and involving people in the process of development. Lastly, a great coach uses passion and **emotions** expressed through their personality and enabling behaviours to motivate those that they coach. They have a mindset that they pass on to others to train others to be productive in their work.

Chapter 4 Purpose is expressed through cognitive, physical and emotional attributes

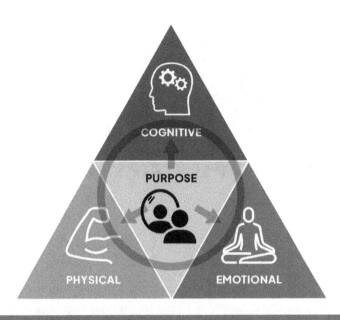

	INDIVIDUAL	ORGANIZATION
PURPOSE	Individual purpose and motivation True self	Clarity and uniqueness of identity, purpose and vision.
COGNITIVE	Competence and skills Reasoning/critical thinking	Differentiating talent and capability.
PHYSICAL	Physical health Rhythms of work and rest	Aligned and empowering organization design. Client centric processes.
EMOTIONAL	Feelings, preferences, self-expression and sense of wellbeing	Culture (mindset, values, and behaviours).

FIGURE 5
Expression of purpose through physical,
emotional and cognitive attributes

APPLE AS AN EXAMPLE OF A LIVING ORGANIZATION

In a similar way, we can see the organization as a macrocosm of the individual. Take the example of Apple Inc, whose core vision (**purpose**) is "to make the best products on earth, and to leave the world better than we found it." In our household, my wife and daughters are deeply attached to their Apple iPads and iPhones because they are so accessible, easy to use and beautifully designed. A great deal of thought has gone into the connection between the users and the device, and this has built a depth of customer loyalty to Apple products.

Apple's vision (purpose) statement has the following elements:

1. Making the best products
2. The world as the target market
3. Leaving the world better

The vision statement's point about making "the best products" requires Apple to align its strategic objectives for the business purpose of achieving excellence. To make the best products (like iPhones) Apple needs the best organization, resources and capabilities. For example, this corporate vision statement makes Apple's operations management apply high standards for productivity and efficiency. The various areas or divisions of the organization must continually improve to protect the business against competitors that are also continually enhancing their respective organizations and information technologies.

This high-quality standard also applies to apps for Apple's operating systems (iOS, iPadOS and macOS).

The term "Earth" in this corporate vision statement means that the company's strategic purposes and objectives aim for excellence at the global level of industries, in this case, consumer electronics. As a result, Apple's marketing mix (the 4Ps)[29] and marketing strategy target the international market for consumer electronics and online services, corresponding to the multinational presence of Apple's stores. This global scope implies that the company develops its products, such as smartphones and laptops, to cater to the diverse needs of customers worldwide.

Apple's vision statement also guides its operations to "leave the world better," which implies satisfying the stakeholders of the business. The company's purpose in stakeholder management focuses on achieving a net benefit for the world through IT and related services. Thus, this vision statement influences Apple's corporate social responsibility; environmental, social and governance; and corporate citizenship efforts towards minimizing environmental impacts and contributing solutions to the world's problems.

HOW IS APPLE'S CORE PURPOSE EXPRESSED?

Apple has a distinctive organizational culture that engages people cognitively, physically and emotionally, releasing creativity and innovation. The company's cultural features focus on maintaining a high level of innovation that involves workers' creativity and a mindset that challenges conventions and standards, such as in consumer electronics design. Apple's IT business depends on cultural support and coherence, which are determinants of competitiveness and industry leadership, especially in addressing aggressive and rapid technological innovation and product development.

Key characteristics of Apple's culture include:

- **Excellence** – Apple's policy is to hire the best people, apply strong performance expectations and reward excellence, particularly in areas such as software design.
- **Creativity** – Apple's management favours creativity above employees' knowledge, skills and abilities as part of selection and advancement. This leads to different ways of approaching consumer electronics product design and development processes.
- **Innovation** – Apple is frequently appraised as one of the most innovative companies in the world. It trains and motivates its employees to innovate in terms of individual work performance and how they contribute ideas to product development, design and other processes.
- **Secrecy** – Apple has a secretive culture to prevent theft of proprietary information or intellectual property, such as designs for the

next generation of the iPhone. This also enables Apple to maximize its leading edge against competitors.
- **Challenging** – This feature is linked to Steve Jobs and his combative approach to leadership. He was known to randomly challenge employees to ensure that they had what it took to work at Apple. He had a challenging and often critical style that brought out the best in some but also frustrated many who left the company.[30]

At the heart of Apple's success is the connection between organizational purpose and employee commitment (**emotional**). At the heart of Apple was the company's purpose and Steve Jobs' vision. Recruitment and leadership were focused on the fit between people and a vision of the future. As Jobs himself said *"Leadership is having a vision, being able to articulate that vision so the people around you can understand it and getting a consensus on a common vision."*

Apple's organizational structure (**physical**) combines a hierarchical layout with divisional elements and some dual reporting between divisions and central functions, adapting traditional business structures to its unique needs. The hierarchy, reminiscent of a 'spoke-and-hub' model, centralized decision-making around Jobs in the past, but under Tim Cook it has evolved to promote greater collaboration and autonomy between various departments, including software and hardware teams. This change reflects a slight shift towards a less rigid structure, though the company maintains its core hierarchical framework, with Cook at the centre and senior vice presidents managing functional business areas.

The company's structure also features product-based divisions, where senior vice presidents oversee different products or components, aligning with a divisional organizational structure. This set-up aids in the management of specific products, such as iOS, macOS and hardware technologies, directly influencing Apple's marketing and distribution strategies.

Apple has particular capabilities (**cognitive**) that enable it to keep its pre-eminent position in the market. The most notable are:

- Strong marketing and branding
- Premium pricing approach
- Effective and rapid innovation processes

Apple is one of the most valuable and strongest brands in the world. In addition, its marketing mix (the 4Ps) involves a premium pricing strategy, which comes with high profit margins. Moreover, Apple's competitive strategy and intensive growth strategies involve rapid innovation. Effective innovation processes enable the business to keep abreast of the latest technologies to ensure it has competitive advantages. The capacity for rapid innovation comes from Apple's strong innovation culture (company culture) and its recruitment profile (smart, innovative individuals).

EFFECTIVE TEAMS HAVE A HUMAN-CENTRIC PATTERN

As we have seen from Apple, effective organizations reflect a fundamentally human-centric pattern of health. We also see this pattern reflected at the level of teams, particularly leadership teams.

At a nuclear energy firm with around 2,000 employees, I worked with the leadership team around the challenge of becoming a focused 'enterprise leadership team' with a clear, shared purpose. Many of the team were new to the firm, with different life and work experiences, although they were all drawn to the unique challenges of the industry (nuclear), the location (a remote area of Scotland) and the future (a merger with a much larger enterprise). They didn't know each other much beyond their day-to-day work, focusing on the functions they led.

To shift this dynamic from individual functions to the overall enterprise, we focused on the following five aspects (also summarized in *Figure 6* on the next page) that research has demonstrated are key to effective leadership teams:

- Shared purpose and goals (**purpose**)
- Strong trust and collaboration between individuals (**emotional**)
- Diversity and integration of complementary skills (**cognitive**)
- Effective ways of working (**physical**)
- Ongoing cycle of learning and development (**growth mindset** – a term that will be explored further in *Chapter 8*)[31]

These aspects are associated with activating a shared team purpose through the three aspects (physical, emotional and cognitive) introduced previously in *Figure 5*.

KEY

Growth — Link back to characteristics from *Figure 5*

1. **SHARED PURPOSE AND GOALS**
   The 'heart of the team' is focused on shared purpose, goals and values. Measures are oriented towards an aligned set of outcomes.

2. **RELEASE TRUST**
   By getting to know each other beyond our roles, we develop empathy and build trust over time, on a foundation of psychological safety.

3. **DIVERSITY AND INTEGRATION**
   We welcome the various team members' contributions and capabilities, through understanding different strengths and how they work together.

4. **WAYS OF WORKING**
   Effective ways of working are based on analysis of how the team works to create collaboration and alignment.

5. **GROWTH MINDSET**
   We focus on both individual and team learning, to not only propel growth but also keep the team striving for excellence.

FIGURE 6
Building an effective 'living' leadership team

The first step in aligning a leadership team focuses on **uncovering their shared purpose**. Most leadership teams are really 'teams of managers' who are focused on their individual functions (e.g. operations, sales, finance) rather than acting as an 'enterprise leadership team' with a single shared purpose. In this case, the operations director was trying to make operations more reliable and run to highly quality standards. Meanwhile, the finance director was trying to reduce staff costs, and the CEO was focused on how the firm worked with its customers. I helped them uncover their primary purpose, which was: "to provide reliable, safe processing of materials for our customers efficiently." Each of the functional directors had a part to play in a single outcome rather than each dancing to a different tune.

Once teams have a shared purpose and ambition, it becomes possible for everyone to pull in the same direction. There were energetic discussions among the leadership team that led them to uncover this shared purpose. In the process, they began to understand their need for one another and **release trust**. This trust needs to go further than a pure task focus and involve team members understanding how each other thinks and works best. This leadership team shared their career stories and motivations (aided by some psychometric diagnostics to reveal different types and drivers) so they could develop empathy for one another and work in harmony.

In machine mindset organizations, people are seen as cogs that can simply be inserted where required, whereas a living organization mindset reveals the importance of understanding colleagues as people with complementary strengths. This process of sharing and assessment led the leadership team to share their strengths, their motivations and the competencies they brought to the team. I helped them ask an important question: "Do we have the right balance of skills in our team to deliver on our overall purpose?" They discovered they had a tendency to focus on concepts and lacked a degree of pragmatism. This was leading them to over-rely on the operations director and spend a lot of time in leadership team meetings talking about ideas rather than delivery plans. As a result, they split the role of the operations director (who already had a large team covering a number of areas) into two roles and brought a new member onto the team with strong delivery skills. They then had a **team with diverse and complementary skills**.

The leadership team was now stronger and more focused and had built a sense of trust. However, their meetings still had a lot of talk and a limited amount of action. They needed to find **new ways of working** that included clear meeting objectives, clarity of governance and a cadence that would drive work forwards. A fortnightly cycle of leadership meetings covered strategy review and oversight, operational decision-making, financial matters and people management. The cycle was rationalized so that the key meetings took up no more than half a day per week, with time released to focus on implementing outcomes from these sessions.

The leadership team started to work more effectively, with greater focus and trust. However, change is not automatic and new meeting rhythms take time to get embedded. The team needed to embrace a **growth mindset**. Therefore, I spent time in selected meetings observing how people were working together, giving feedback (individually and to the group) to help build up the team's capabilities. The same diagnostics used at the start of the process were re-run to see how the leadership team themselves, their direct reports, the board and the firm's customers felt about the team's effectiveness.

Because all the dimensions of the team (purpose, cognitive, physical and emotional) were addressed, change became permanent and was reflected in improved productivity and engagement. Taking a human-centric organizational approach ensured that change went below the temporary, surface level and became part of 'how we do things round here.'

CHARACTERISTICS OF HEALTHY LIVING ORGANIZATIONS

As the above example of the engineering firm's safety challenges demonstrates, when we recognize that teams are living groups rather than static mechanistic structures, then change can happen. I have illustrated throughout this chapter that this dynamic works at the individual level, the team level, the organization level and, ultimately, at the cross-organizational level. While the reality is slightly different at each level, the same principles apply. Return to *Figure 5* for a reminder of how identity is expressed at the individual and team levels in terms of purpose as well as cognitively, physically and emotionally.

KEY LEARNING POINTS

- Individuals have a unique purpose, which they express cognitively, emotionally and physically.

- All of the dimensions of an individual need to be 'healthy' for a person to live a fruitful and fulfilling life – good mental health, emotional wellbeing and physical health.

- In the same way, teams and organizations need to uncover their purpose and bring it to life through their cognitive abilities, physical being and emotions.

- Teams can support their health through establishing their purpose within the whole organization; they should have trust, diversity and integration, effective ways of working and a growth mindset.

APPLICATION EXERCISE

Try applying the living organization dimensions to your own team using these questions:

EFFECTIVE LEADERSHIP TEAM CHARACTERISTIC	HELPFUL QUESTIONS TO ASK
Clear shared purpose and ambition (purpose)	• Do we have alignment as a leadership team, around our purpose and what success looks like? • Are we committed to a single shared aim as a team, or do we each have our own aims?
Strong trust and collaboration between individuals (emotional)	• Do we have a sense of 'psychological safety' to freely express our thoughts and ideas when together? • Do we know one another beyond our immediate work roles (in terms of our interests and motivations)?
Diverse and complementary competencies (cognitive)	• Do we understand each other's talents and strengths? • Do we play to each other's strengths and complementary talents in the way that we work together? • Do we lack diversity on the team?
Effective ways of working (physical)	• Do we have an effective and well-established pattern of meetings and ways of relating? • Do we have clarity about how decisions are made and who is responsible?
Ongoing cycle of learning and development (growth mindset)	• Are we actively learning and growing, as leaders, and helping others to do so? • How do we support our teams in their own learning and growth?

CHAPTER 5

UNIQUENESS (DIFFERENTIATION AND SIMILARITY) OF CAPABILITIES

> **Living Organization Characteristic 3:
> Capability Based**
>
> - All cells have the same basic elements (stem cells), but they specialize to perform different functions.
> - Organizations have core and unique capabilities/gifts that support their identity.

A CREATIVE LEARNING STRATEGY

We had become the 'Three Musketeers.' A colleague and I had been working closely as consultants with Dawn, the director of learning and capability for a UK government department employing over 70,000 people, for a couple of years on smaller pieces of work. We had won a major new contract to deliver the department's five-year learning strategy. It was a Tuesday morning, and we were in a spacious room in the department's HQ, with the three of us talking about how we could engage a large group of (internal and external) stakeholders in developing a much broader learning approach than the 'white board, slides and instructor' approach that had been the standard formula over the past five years. There was a natural chemistry between the three of us because of our previous work together and our appreciation of the different gifts we brought to the table.

Dawn, in her usual inimitable fashion, started provocatively by saying, "Our approach is so boring and conventional. We talk about embracing digital while delivering old material in dark rooms about topics that have little relevance to the day-to-day work and challenges of our staff. We need some inspiration, and we need to get people excited about it." Phil started to relate his experience of helping Cisco develop its learning academy, which embraced many of the great technology innovations, ranging from Webex Meetings to telepresence to an emerging Networking Academy concept. Dawn countered that "it sounds great but we're a government department, not Cisco." I provided some more pragmatic web and professional community learning solution examples that Phil and I had recently delivered to a large oil and gas company. We all agreed that we'd like to open the eyes of staff, managers, learning professionals and a couple of the key directors to the possibility of a very different future.

We debated for a further hour. Dawn would bring a challenge drawing on her desire for excellence and innovation while maintaining a degree of realism about what could be achieved in the governmental context. Phil pushed innovative and strategic ideas into the conversation. I acted as a voice to both provoke and integrate the ideas into an initial requirement and a potential process for engaging these diverse stakeholders around a 'vision of learning in the future.' We bounced our ideas off one another. There was a real sense of energy and almost a suspense of time (the two hours went quickly!) as we cohered around a concept for how the project could deliver both a vision of the future and a realistic strategy to deliver the vision. We were a great team, bringing both similar, strategic mindsets and different skills.

Over the following few weeks, we agreed an approach that involved taking stakeholders to organizations that were leading the field in learning, including a global airline, a multinational oil and gas company, a professional services organization and an innovative government-owned enterprise. These best-practice visits included making highlight videos of the visits and writing short insight reports. We held an academic roundtable using World Café-style facilitation to draw out inspiration and ideas about the latest theory and practice around learning strategy, methods and technology.[32]

It all culminated in a big event at an innovation centre with more than 50 stakeholders from across the organization (and a few external people) bringing together five strategic themes (and practical activity) for the future of learning in the organization. One collaborator was my colleague Janet, who had deep expertise in learning from leading a large learning function at a global airline and who shared best-practice examples and inspiration with the group. We also had an artistic facilitator who helped the group to capture three learning stories for a director, a manager and a staff member in the future organization. These were captured as cartoon-style 'day in the life' stories of these people and their new experiences of learning as part of their day-to-day work. Alongside this, the strategic themes were built out into a 'learning strategy map' and strategy document that mapped these themes into practical initiatives and concepts built on the outputs of the innovation centre event. Much of the communication to wider leaders and stakeholders drew on the creative outputs, such as the 'day in the life' cartoons, to communicate this vision.

The day's impact was only possible because we brought together a diverse team (including both consultants and clients) around a common purpose. We had sufficient similarity to, and knowledge of, one another while bringing different capabilities to achieve an outstanding result.

WHAT CAN WE LEARN FROM OUR OWN BODIES?

Our human bodies have both similarity and differentiation among their cells and organs. This enables them to both deliver important functions and respond to the current context. A good example is the functioning of the human immune system, particularly in how blood cells operate together.

SIMILARITY: COMMON ORIGIN AND BASIC STRUCTURES

All blood cells originate from the same type of cell in the bone marrow, known as stem cells. This common origin underscores the similarity across different types of blood cells. They all share certain basic cellular components, such as a cell membrane, cytoplasm and, in most cases, a nucleus (except in mature red blood cells). These shared features allow them to function effectively within the blood and immune system.

DIFFERENTIATION: SPECIALIZED BLOOD CELLS

From this common lineage, blood cells differentiate into various specialized types, each with distinct functions:

- **Red blood cells (erythrocytes)** – These cells are specialized for oxygen transport. They lose their nucleus during maturation to make more room for haemoglobin, the protein that binds oxygen. This

structural differentiation allows them to efficiently carry oxygen from the lungs to other parts of the body.
- **White blood cells (leukocytes)** – These are involved in defending the body against infections and foreign invaders. White blood cells are further differentiated into several types, including lymphocytes (which are crucial for the adaptive immune response), neutrophils and monocytes (which are key players in the innate immune response). Each type of white blood cell has a specialized function, from killing bacteria to creating antibodies.
- **Platelets** – Although not cells in the traditional sense (they are fragments of larger cells called megakaryocytes), platelets play a critical role in blood clotting. When bleeding occurs, platelets aggregate to form clots, preventing excessive blood loss.

SYSTEMIC COORDINATION: INTEGRATED FUNCTIONING

Despite their differences, all these blood cells work together seamlessly. For instance, when an injury occurs, platelets gather at the site to form a clot. At the same time, white blood cells rush to the area to prevent infection and promote healing. This coordinated response showcases how different cells and organs in the body interact in a unified, systemic manner to maintain health and respond to challenges.

This example of blood cells encapsulates the broader principles of similarity and differentiation within the human body. Cells share common features and origins, yet they diversify to fulfil specialized roles, all while working together to support the overall functioning and health of the body.

THE CONCEPT OF CAPABILITIES:
BRINGING TOGETHER UNIQUE STRENGTHS

Organizations are made up of people. People, like stem cells in the body, have many common characteristics, including basic needs such as physical requirements (food, shelter), safety, belonging, self-esteem and significance. They also have common capabilities, such as movement, relating to others, solving problems and creating new concepts. However, people are wonderfully varied and different, just like the cells in our bodies are. Our world contains great academics like Stephen Hawking, amazing athletes like Michael Jordan, wonderful artists like Salvador Dali and businesspeople like Sir Richard Branson. Each person brings a different set of skills, knowledge and experience, beyond these common characteristics – this is the specialization of people.

Great teams manage to incorporate and harness people's complementary skills to achieve outstanding results. At the time of writing in the UK, Manchester City Football Club has recently won the Premier League for the fourth time in a row – the first time this has ever been done. Their manager, Pep Guardiola, has managed to integrate the 'goal machine' striker, Erling Haaland, with the midfield 'opportunity creators' like Kevin De Bruyne and Phil Foden and the fast ball distribution of the goalkeeper, Ederson.[33] It is this combination of capabilities that creates a strong team.

In the world of organizations and teams, we see this combination of strategic capabilities replicated to build unbeatable firms. Most people will know the firm Lego. Lego is a globally renowned Danish toy company, founded in 1932, that manufactures a popular line of interlocking plastic bricks that allow for creative and imaginative construction play. Lego has combined a set of capabilities to be highly successful, including:

- **Product innovation across design and development** – Lego has created new lines of business, such as movies, video games and amusement parks.
- **Brand strength built on community engagement** – Lego Ideas and Lego Education are examples of how the company has engaged with both adults and children to form a strong attachment to Lego products and the brand.
- **Global supply chain and manufacturing efficiency** – in order to bring the Lego system to market affordably and profitably, the company has needed to build a supply chain that can make and deliver to countries as disparate as China and the USA.

Just like a great team or individual, successful organizations work out what their strategic capabilities are and how to harness them together to deliver outstanding experiences for clients and customers.

HOW DO CAPABILITIES WORK TOGETHER?

We need first to understand what we mean by a 'capability.'[34] I define a capability as the combination of people, processes, technology, organization and ways of working that enables a firm to deliver an outcome. For example, we might say that Google has the capability to rapidly search digital information, which involves technology, processes and human coding skills.

Like the human body, capabilities need to be combined into a whole system to provide their unique contribution to the world. I call this a 'capabilities set.' This is a set of capabilities working in harmony, like the football team example earlier, to deliver strategic outcomes. Therefore, I define a capabilities set as the combination of a small number of reinforcing capabilities that, together, create a valuable outcome.

Maturing human beings, as they grow up, become more and more aware of their strengths and weaknesses, allowing them to take on jobs and activities that play to their unique combination of capabilities – their personal 'capabilities set.' One child discovers they have a set of creative and design gifts and ends up working for a fashion house in design. Another discovers great strengths in maths and problem-solving and decides to take on an engineering career. It is also clear that both people and organizations take time to discover and hone their capabilities.

AMAZON:
BRINGING UNIQUE CAPABILITIES TOGETHER TO CREATE THE WORLD'S BIGGEST ONLINE SHOP

Many readers will use Amazon as their online retailer of choice. In *Chapter 3*, we explored the idea of clarity around a company's purpose. Under the leadership of Jeff Bezos, Amazon is crystal clear on its purpose, which is "to be Earth's most customer-centric company, where customers can find and discover anything they want to buy online." By starting with a clarity of purpose and then moving on to strategy, it is possible to understand the capabilities that underpin their success (see *Table 4* on the next page).

Purpose	Amazon seeks to be Earth's most customer-centric company, where customers can find and discover anything they want to buy online
Customer interface design	Development and evolution of digital pages that are attractive, are easy to use, and have sophisticated search and payment features.
Supply chain management	Management of specialized warehouses and distribution networks incorporating many partners, vendors and suppliers to form a timely and reliable network.
Customer relationship and relevance	Depth of (data-driven) customer insight to notify customers of links to and recommendations for relevant and well-rated products alongside rapid resolution of customer issues.
Technological innovation	Ongoing evolution of the online platform with features such as one-click instant ordering and cloud computing services.

TABLE 4
Amazon's capabilities set[35]

When we go to the Amazon website to buy a product like a popular business book, we see all of these capabilities in action together. It is quick and simple to find the business book through the search bar by entering something like "Collins Built to Last." In under a second, we are presented with a list of books and find that *Built to Last* by Jim Collins and Jerry Porras is the first on the list. This is the **customer interface design** capability. Next, we are offered a variety of formats and easy, one-click ordering (**technological innovation** capability). From the same screen, we can jump to the profiles of the authors, so we can see other interesting business books by them. There is also a list of "Frequently bought together" books and "Products related to this item," which may be relevant to us based on our similarity to other customers (**customer relationship and relevance** capability). When we have placed our order, we will then typically receive the book within one day, particularly with Amazon Prime. This draws on the world-class **supply chain management** capability that Amazon has built.

HOW CAN WE START BUILDING OUR ORGANIZATION'S STRATEGIC CAPABILITIES?

Amazon's business wasn't built in a day, but it did start with a clarity of purpose and identity, a concept we examined in *Chapter 3*. There are a series of questions that an organization must answer to define, shape and build each of the capabilities it needs to succeed in its market. These questions are shown in *Figure 7*.

1. What is our purpose and customer value proposition?
2. What is the set of capabilities that enable strategy delivery?
3. For each capability:
   a. What is it?
   b. Why is it valuable?
   c. How is it different from today?
   d. What does it look like in action?
   e. What is required to make it happen?
4. For all of the capabilities:
   a. What investment do we need to make, and can we justify it?
   b. How do we phase the introduction of services to maximize growth and impact and minimize our initial set-up costs?
   c. Are there different ways of realizing our capabilities – through partnering, buying an existing firm with those capabilities or working with an adviser who has delivered these successfully in the past?

FIGURE 7
Questions to ask to shape your organization's capabilities set

STARLING BANK:
A DETAILED CASE STUDY OF CAPABILITIES IN PRACTICE

Let's take a look at this topic in more detail for a bank that is seeking to provide an outstanding online digital experience for businesses. The example I have chosen is Starling Bank, which was founded by Anne Boden, a former COO of Allied Irish Banks, in 2014. Noting that customers were dissatisfied with traditional business banking, Boden saw an opportunity to create a fully digital bank offering innovative services through mobile and web platforms.

We'll use the capability question framework in *Figure 7* to look at how Starling Bank is very different from traditional banks (like Allied Irish Banks) and the new capability set that underpins this.

Firstly, there was **clarity on purpose and the customer value proposition**, focused on four areas:

1. **Seamless digital experience** – Starling Bank has a fully digital, mobile-first banking platform that offers convenience and ease of use, allowing customers to manage their finances anytime, anywhere.

2. **Real-time financial insights** – The bank offers real-time notifications, spending analytics and budgeting tools to help customers gain better control and understanding of their financial situation (see *Figure 8* on the next page).

3. **Fee-free, integrated international transactions** – The bank provides fee-free spending abroad and competitive exchange rates, making it an attractive choice for international travellers.
4. **Integrated financial marketplace** – The bank provides access to a wide range of third-party financial services through the Starling Marketplace, allowing customers to manage all their financial needs in one place.

FIGURE 8
Starling Bank's account concept[36]

In order to deliver on this purpose and proposition, it was clear to Anne and her team that Starling Bank would require a different set of capabilities from traditional, typically high street-based, banks. Naturally there was the essential ingredient of Starling Bank getting its banking licences from the Prudential Regulation Authority and the Financial Conduct Authority in 2016, in advance of its launch. However, the initial growth followed a very different path from that of traditional banks with the launch of its first product, a mobile personal current account, in March 2017, which included features like real-time notifications, spending insights and fee-free spending abroad. This was followed by the launch in 2018 of business accounts for small and medium-sized enterprises. Starling Bank also launched its Marketplace, an integration platform where customers could access third-party financial products and services.

Moving on to the next item in the capability question framework, what did the bank do to successfully build an award-winning digital banking experience? What was the **organizational capabilities set** required (question 2 from *Figure 7*)? And, for each capability, what were the specific elements (question 3a) and what was their **value** (question 3b)?

1. **Agile development and innovation**
    > **Continuous improvement** – Starling Bank operates with an agile development approach, enabling rapid iteration and continuous improvement of its products and services.
    Value – This allows the bank to swiftly respond to customer feedback and market changes.
    > **Innovation culture** – The organization fosters a culture of innovation, encouraging employees to experiment with new ideas and technologies.
    Value – Ongoing enhancement of the banking experience.

2. **Data-driven decision-making**
    > **Advanced analytics** – Starling leverages advanced data analytics to gain insights into customer behaviour, optimize its operations and identify new business opportunities.
    Value – This data-driven approach ensures that decisions are based on accurate, real-time information.
    > **Personalization** – By using customer data, Starling can personalize services and offers.
    Value – Enhancement of customer satisfaction and loyalty.

3. **Robust technology infrastructure:**
   › **Scalable cloud-based systems** – Starling's IT infrastructure is built on scalable, cloud-based systems that ensure high availability, security and performance.
   Value – This infrastructure supports the bank's rapid growth and the ability to handle increasing transaction volumes.
   › **Cybersecurity** – The bank prioritizes cybersecurity, employing advanced measures to protect customer data and financial transactions from cyber threats.
   Value – Customers are attracted and retained by the bank's reputation for security.

4. **Regulatory compliance and risk management:**
   › **Strong compliance framework** – Starling has established a strong compliance framework to meet regulatory requirements and ensure ethical business practices.
   Value – More freedom granted by regulators to expand into new services.
   › **Risk management** – The bank employs comprehensive risk management strategies to identify, assess and mitigate risks, including financial risks, operational risks and reputational risks, ensuring the stability and reliability of its services.
   Value – De-risking operations.

5. **Customer-centric operations:**
   › **Customer support excellence** – Starling is committed to providing excellent customer support, available 24/7 via its mobile app.
   Value – Customers receive timely and effective assistance, driving increased customer satisfaction.
   › **Feedback integration** – The bank actively seeks and integrates customer feedback into its development process.
   Value – This ensures that products and services are closely aligned with customer needs and expectations.

This system of five organizational capabilities enables Starling Bank to deliver a superior banking experience, maintain regulatory compliance and continue innovating in the competitive financial services industry.

It takes a depth of market and customer research and understanding to work out what a compelling value proposition is, and which four or five strategic organizational capabilities will enable a new or resurgent firm to succeed in its market. This is what questions 1, 2, 3a and 3b look at. We can then unpack each of the strategic organization capabilities by answering questions 3c, 3d and 3e for each capability:

c. How is it different from today?
d. What does it look like in action?
e. What is required to make it happen?

Table 5 gives an insight into how we might unpack these questions for Starling Bank for the agile development and innovation capability. We can see that Starling has a very different mindset in building out this capability, thinking like a fast-moving product-based technology company rather than a traditional bank. There is a heavy emphasis on software engineering talent working in cross-functional product-based teams (e.g. a product team delivering the core online digital user experience) with people with other required skills (such as customer experience design, product management and commerce). This is underpinned by a state-of-the-art, cloud-based technology infrastructure. The result is rapid, often daily improvements in the customer experience, which a traditional business bank finds very difficult to replicate – hard-wiring in a strategic advantage for Starling Bank.

Chapter 5 — Uniqueness (differentiation and similarity) of capabilities

	STARLING BANK[37]	**TRADITIONAL BUSINESS BANK**[38]
People and teams	Focuses heavily on hiring **top software engineering talent**, with a significant portion of its workforce being software engineers. Employs **cross-functional teams** with diverse expertise in engineering, marketing, data science and customer experience, which promotes rapid innovation and inclusive development.	Follows a **more traditional structure with specialized roles** in banking operations, customer service, risk management and compliance. Engineering and tech **roles are typically separate** from customer-facing roles, resulting in slower innovation cycles.
Processes	Uses **agile development methodologies**, allowing for rapid iteration and implementation of new features based on customer feedback. **Code is deployed daily**, ensuring continuous updates and improvements.	Follows a **waterfall development approach** with longer cycles. Changes and updates are less frequent, and the implementation of **new features can take months** or even years.
Structures	Built its entire technology stack in-house, providing greater control and flexibility. It is a **product-based organization** (oriented around specific products and services), which facilitates faster decision-making and shared ownership.	Relies on legacy systems and third-party packages, which can lead to slower innovation and flexibility. It has a **traditional hierarchical structure with separate departments**, resulting in slower decision-making processes.
Technology	Uses a **fully cloud-based infrastructure**, enhancing scalability, security and innovation capabilities. It was an early adopter of **open APIs** (application programming interfaces), facilitating integration with other financial services and promoting a connected ecosystem.	Uses a **mix of on-premises and cloud solutions**, with a slower transition to a fully cloud-based infrastructure. They have a more cautious approach to open APIs and integration, which often results in a **less connected and slower-to-adapt ecosystem.**

TABLE 5
Unpacking the agile development and innovation capability of Starling Bank versus a traditional business bank

Finally, commercial realism needs to be brought to bear in the delivery of this customer provision (question 4 of *Figure 7*). This involves tackling important questions, including:

a. For all of the capabilities, what investment do we need to make, and can we justify it?
b. How do we phase the introduction of services to maximize growth and impact, and minimize our initial set-up costs?
c. Are there different ways of realizing our capabilities – through partnering, buying an existing firm with those capabilities or working with an adviser who has delivered these successfully in the past?

CAPABILITIES AND THE OPPORTUNITIES OF ARTIFICIAL INTELLIGENCE

Many books and articles have been written about artificial intelligence (AI) and the power of tools like ChatGPT and robots to replace humans in workplaces. However, evidence points to AI being more about extending human capabilities than completing replacing them. In *Chapter 1*, we were introduced to the contrast between a mechanistic automotive firm that had got stuck in the past (AP Products) and the innovative and forward-looking approach of Nissan at its Sunderland manufacturing plant. Here, we can see examples of how Nissan has used AI to supplement and extend its capabilities.

As we saw earlier, Nissan's core capabilities include advanced manufacturing, lean production and quality assurance, all underpinned by continuous innovation. At its Sunderland plant, Nissan has used AI to strengthen these core capabilities, automating routine tasks, augmenting worker roles and creating new capabilities:

- **Advanced manufacturing** – AI-powered robotic arms automate welding, painting and assembly processes for models such as the Nissan Qashqai. These systems operate at high speeds and ensure consistent quality, enhancing Nissan's ability to meet high demand efficiently.
- **Lean production** – AI-driven logistics robots support lean processes, transporting parts across the plant autonomously. This reduces idle time and ensures that assembly lines remain uninterrupted, making production more efficient.

- **Quality assurance** – AI augments quality control with computer vision systems that inspect parts for defects far faster and more accurately than human workers alone. For instance, these systems immediately detect any paint imperfections or assembly misalignments, allowing human inspectors to focus on trend analysis and corrective action.
- **Creating new capabilities** – AI adoption has led Nissan to establish new roles such as 'AI systems engineer' and 'data analytics specialist.' These positions manage and optimize AI systems, ensuring they are focused on improving production processes and extending core capabilities that drive productivity and lean operations.[39]

The example of Nissan provides a lens we can use when looking at AI and its impact in our organizations. Rather than just getting excited about the clever things that AI can do (like writing a Shakespearean sonnet about the English weather!), a good way to evaluate the benefits of AI is to look at three areas of impact:

- **Automation** – Some skills and roles are replaced by technologies such as robotic process automation (like the automated logistics of the Nissan plant) and other forms of digitization.
- **Augmentation** – Many roles change and are made more effective through technology and new ways of working, such as augmented visual inspection of manufactured parts for flaws and errors.
- **Addition** – New roles are required to build a company's future. This might include roles to program robots and computerized equipment to better deliver the results.

KEY LEARNING POINTS

- Our human bodies demonstrate both similarity and differentiation among their cells and organs.

- Humans have and are able to develop common capabilities (e.g. relating to others, exercising) and unique capabilities (e.g. creative design) to express their identity, and this enables them to play an important part in the world and be rewarded for using these capabilities.

- In the same way, teams and organizations succeed by being clear in the capabilities they need to express their purpose and identity; these capabilities, like those of individuals, are developed and honed over time.

- A capability can be defined as the "combination of people, processes, technology, organization and ways of working that enables a firm to deliver an outcome."

- A capabilities set can be defined as "the combination of a small number of reinforcing capabilities that, together, allow an organization to create a valuable outcome."

- Successful organizations, such as Google and Amazon, have clarified a small number of capabilities (typically four or five) that they wish to be the best at.

- AI can be used to enhance capabilities in three ways:
  - **Automation** of routine processes – such as tracking packages.
  - **Augmentation** of existing processes – such as providing virtual reality visualizations of designs that humans can 'walk through.'
  - **Addition** of new capabilities – such as automatically creating new music playlists that a user might like based on other observed preferences.

APPLICATION EXERCISE

Think about your own organization, or one you know well, and answer the following questions for it, using the supporting prompts to help you at each stage.

1. What is our purpose and customer value proposition?

2. What is the set of capabilities that will enable us to deliver our strategy?

3. For each capability, review and complete the questions shown in the table. There are some further prompt questions to help you. In addition, I advise you to look back at the Starling Bank example for inspiration:

QUESTION	PROMPT QUESTIONS
What is the capability?	• What are the inputs? • What are the outputs? • What are the key activities? Advice: • Be clear on outputs first • Break the capability down into specific activities that are relevant to your market (not generic)
Why is it valuable?	• How does it ensure value to the customer? • How does it ensure that we can deliver profitably? • How does it reduce our risk? • How does it avoid unnecessary handoffs and distance from the customer?

QUESTION	PROMPT QUESTIONS
How is it different from today?	- What are the problems that we face today that this capability enables us to address? - How does it enable our strategic goal(s)? - How does it ensure that we get a competitive advantage by doing things differently from others? - How does it improve or change our relationship with the customer? - What will we need to change?
What does it look like in action?	- What will our teams be doing? - How will they work with suppliers and clients? - Who will do what? - What will our role and scope be?
What is required to make it happen?	- What are the key processes that underpin this capability? - Are new or improved tools and systems needed to support them? - How will team structures and the organization need to change? - What new skills and knowledge are required? - How might we enhance the capability using AI through automation, augmentation or addition of new elements to the capability?

4. Finally, review your approach to delivering the capabilities. For all of the capabilities, look at the business case and implementation approach by answering the following questions:
   a. For all of the capabilities, what investment do we need to make, and can we justify it?
   b. How do we phase the introduction of services to maximize growth and impact and minimize our initial set-up costs?
   c. Are there different ways of realizing our capabilities – through partnering, buying an existing firm with those capabilities or working with an adviser who has delivered these successfully in the past?

CHAPTER 6

EMPOWER – TO ADAPT AND IMPROVE

**Living Organization Characteristic 4:
Living/Adaptive**

- Bodies respond at the local, or sub-system, level (e.g. the digestive system is a local system, capillaries close up when it's cold).

THE ALWAYS-BREAKING PRODUCTION LINE

The drug production plant belonged to a major international pharmaceutical firm. It was located outside a Welsh town that provided a ready source of production staff in an area that had both plenty of land and grants available to support the manufacturing industry. Research and development of the drugs produced at the plant was undertaken at another site until the drug formulation, testing and regulatory approval had been completed. The plant then took the drug formula and turned it into a multi-stage process from synthesis of ingredients to product formulation, pill production and quality control, packaging and labelling, and distribution. My team and I were working with the packaging and labelling teams.

There were four teams of ten people working in parallel, packaging and labelling all the drugs produced at the plant. Each team had a production machine that took a large hopper of pills, which were fed into blister packs (typically containing 20 pills) and then sealed. They were then packed with instructions into prepared boxes. Finally, the packages were printed with the date of production and other key details. Typically, a team of ten people would run a single drug packaging and labelling line, ensuring that there was a ready supply of ingredients (pills, boxes and instructions). They would also undertake checking and quality control. The teams were given production targets and generally worked in a good-humoured way despite the somewhat repetitive nature of the tasks. *Figure 9* shows the packaging line equipment.

FIGURE 9
Drug blister packaging line

However, elements of the production machinery would break down from time to time. The pill feed would become jammed and had to be stopped. The labelling machine would occasionally shred the labels, because they had been misloaded or because there was a faulty, non-standard size set of labels. The whole line would grind to a halt. If the fault wasn't minor, an engineer would be called. The team had got used to putting the kettle on and sitting down for a cup of tea, knowing that it might take 20–40 minutes for an engineer to come across and repair the fault. Nothing could be done in the meantime. It was a cause of frustration for a team that had targets. Over time, many people left, as they grew disengaged as a result of being held to targets that they couldn't control. Some of the production machines were old so they typically broke down more often and the team involved was seen as "poor performing."

When we were engaged, this was one element of the production process we were looking at. As a consulting team, we diagnosed the basic source of the issue. The team were responsible for a process that they didn't have full control over – they could improve the way they ran the production machinery but couldn't fix breakdowns. They were given goals where they didn't have control over the means to achieve them.

We agreed that we would try a new approach. Rather than having a central engineering group, there was an engineer embedded in each of the teams who could fix the faults as they occurred. Each team now had production, quality control and engineering staff. The improvement was immediate, with production levels improving by over 10%. Over time, the teams found ways to improve things further. They found the same faults occurring again and again, so the engineers looked into preventative maintenance (ensuring the machines were serviced ahead of any faults occurring) and the teams began having regular daily and weekly sessions where they discussed other proactive improvements they could make. Now they had the right mix of skills to 'plan, do and improve' the work cycle.

OUR BODIES KNOW HOW TO ADAPT

The problem at the drug production plant stemmed from the fact that the local production teams were not able to address their part of the process, improving and adapting how it was undertaken. Our bodies don't have this problem – adaptation is built into our being. An example can be found in muscles. Muscles adapt through a process known as hypertrophy. We observe this process in action when we see people working out down at our local gym:

- **Initial stimulus** – When a person begins a new exercise routine, such as resistance training (e.g. weightlifting), the muscles in their body experience 'micro-tears' due to the unfamiliar stress. They need to take care they increase the weight they lift sensibly, or these tears become too severe.
- **Inflammatory response** – The body responds to these micro-tears with a process of inflammation that involves the release of growth factors and cytokines (signalling proteins) to repair the damaged muscle fibres.
- **Protein synthesis** – To repair and strengthen the muscle fibres, the body increases protein synthesis. This process involves satellite cells (a type of stem cell found in muscle) that multiply and fuse with existing muscle fibres, adding nuclei and increasing the muscle's capacity to produce new proteins. Keen bodybuilders will often supplement this process with protein shakes and other nutrition.

- **Hypertrophy** – Over time, with consistent exercise, the muscle fibres grow in size (hypertrophy). They thicken as they accumulate more protein filaments (actin and myosin) and increase the size and number of their contractile units (sarcomeres).
- **Improved functionality** – The muscles not only grow larger but also become more efficient at generating force and resisting fatigue. This results in increased strength and endurance.

What can we learn from how the body adapts and grows its muscle capability as exercise is undertaken?

1. **Right conditions** – People need to lift the right level of weights to stretch their capacity without damaging themselves, and they need to lift regularly to achieve growth and development.
   Learning – If we don't have the right team members, leadership and goals then growth won't happen.

2. **Local impact** – People can exercise and develop particular muscles to target the improvement – for instance, to the arm muscles rather than the leg muscles.
   Learning – We can give our local teams a particular focus, which is likely to be different from the focus of the wider system.

3. **Reversibility** – Sadly, anyone who has tried to do regular workouts will recognize how quickly the body returns to its previous, less muscular state! We need to ensure the system is developed and monitored to continue to grow, typically in stages.
   Learning – We need to embed improvements into day-to-day practice.

4. **Need to learn how body responds** – The rate and extent of development (hypertrophy) can vary significantly between individuals due to factors such as genetics, diet, age and overall health.
   Learning – There isn't one 'best practice,' and we need ways to continuously learn.

WHY DOESN'T THIS HAPPEN IN ORGANIZATIONS?

There are two answers to this question. Firstly, it is clear that some improvement and adaptation *does* happen, as evidenced by the prevalence of 'improvement teams,' 'performance excellence frameworks' and 'continuous improvement initiatives.' However, the premise of this book is that many organizations are viewed as machines to be fixed rather than bodies that adapt and grow over time. Typical responses, based on this machine mindset, include:

1. **Best practice** – We assess our process or team against external best practice (e.g. how a leading competitor in the industry undertakes its production process). However, we find this practice works well for them but not for us because their situation and context are different.

2. **Fix and move on** – We create an improvement team, find a solution and then move on. There is an initial improvement but benefits atrophy over time and new problems appear.

3. **Benchmark** – We find an external measure of performance and try to manage to this benchmark (e.g. ratio of HR staff to overall staff) but find the quality of services reduces as staff numbers decrease to fit the benchmark.

4. **Outsource** – Often following benchmarking, it is identified that a service could be outsourced more cheaply while maintaining the same service level. However, this introduces new handoffs and contracting time, which adds an external cost without reducing the internal costs by the level expected.

While there can be value in some of these practices, the fundamental issue is the mentality of 'replacing a cog in the machine' rather than growing and developing capability. Inherent in the former mentality is the drive to reduce the cost of an existing process (efficiency focus) rather than improving what is done (effectiveness focus). We need to 'do the right things right' (effectiveness and efficiency). Our world changes quickly, with new technology, evolving economic conditions and social changes (such as ageing populations), so 'fixing' an existing system is rarely the answer.

HOW CAN WE DO BETTER BY LEARNING FROM OUR OWN BODIES?

By drawing on learning from our own bodies, we can see that sustainable improvement comes from having local control and empowerment. Our muscles can develop independently because the conditions exist for them to grow and develop in response to our gym workouts!

To achieve this for teams, we need to enable them to plan their work, deliver it and improve how it is done. This 'plan, do and improve' cycle requires the right conditions – what I refer to as a 'whole work team.' *Figure 10* shows the basic principles of a whole work team. The team has a well-defined purpose that it is formed to achieve. For instance, a customer account team's purpose might be defined as "nurturing the long-term sales relationship and lifetime value through the supply of services and support." The team does this through account planning (understanding key relationships and how to support them, and setting revenue and service goals), delivering on these activities, and making improvements (measuring net promoter scores, revenue, and customer feedback and satisfaction). Once a team understands the scope of the required activities (that link back to the team purpose), it can determine the required inputs and outputs.

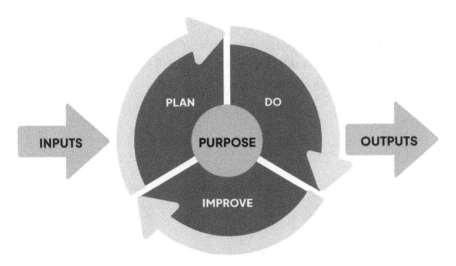

FIGURE 10
Whole work teams have a clear purpose in the plan, do and improve process

While the principle of a whole work team is well defined, this kind of team requires certain characteristics and conditions to deliver effectively (see *Figure 11* on the next page). As previously described, the team needs a clear purpose, so they are clear on why they exist and have the ability (like the drug-packing team at the start of this chapter) to plan, do and improve their work. This means the team needs to be clear on the contribution of each team member and the skills necessary to deliver effectively as part of the drug-packing team. Performance measures need to align with purpose. So, the asset account management team might be measured in terms of net promoter score (indicating they are looking after and retaining their account customers) and long-term revenue (rather than short-term sales, which may jeopardize giving their customers the best long-term benefit).

There are other elements of a whole work team that should not be overlooked. Every member of the team needs to make a contribution under an empowering leader who ensures the team is greater than the sum of its parts, because it is delivering its purpose and continually improving. The team also needs to be at a 'human scale' where good relationships and communication can be maintained. Studies show such teams typically consist of five to twelve members.[40] This size allows for optimal communication, collaboration and decision-making, ensuring that each member can contribute meaningfully while maintaining a manageable level of complexity in team dynamics. Teams within this range are large enough to bring diverse perspectives and skills, but small enough to foster strong relationships and efficient coordination.

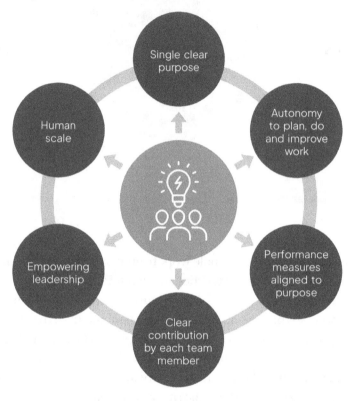

FIGURE 11
Characteristics of a whole work team

To begin the journey to forming such teams, leaders should ask:

1. For the group, what is the purpose and significant output? How would we measure it?
2. What people (skills and roles) do we need in the group to achieve the purpose?
3. What development and tools do the group need to help them innovate and improve?
4. How can the team leader and organization ensure the conditions for continuous improvement?

HEALTHCARE EXAMPLE:
AN ORTHOPAEDIC TREATMENT CENTRE

A close friend had been leading the establishment of a new treatment centre that sought to radically change the way that the UK National Health Service performed routine surgery. This healthcare facility is now the largest joint-replacement centre in the UK and one of the largest in Europe. At the time of writing, it performs around 6,300 procedures a year, with approximately 4,000 of those being joint replacements – such as knee, shoulder and hip replacements. The centre was formed with the vision of delivering world-class care with the latest techniques and technologies to help reduce pain and get people back to normal in as safe and quick a manner as possible.

So, what needed to change? Traditionally, joint replacements (routine, scheduled surgery) were done in the same hospital as acute, emergency procedures. Doctors and nurses were shared across these patients without having a clear purpose to help a group of patients to recover and get back to normal. This led to a task focus, with members of staff doing their own jobs well but without a sense of satisfaction seeing the results of their labours as a team.

When this regular, scheduled (elective) orthopaedic surgery was placed in a separate treatment centre, clinical staff could be formed into teams to deal with the various stages of the patient pathway (see *Figure 12*). For instance, one team deals with the assessment and pre-operative preparation, ensuring that patients have a clear assessment and treatment plan. The operating surgery team is responsible for admission and successful completion of surgery. Each team is responsible for a meaningful change in the state of the patient – allowing them to plan, do and improve the service they are delivering. By using improvement techniques (such as Lean Six Sigma and quality circles, both of which are considered in the next section), they can look at how their stage of the process can be improved. For instance, this includes incorporating new orthopaedic technology from the USA that allows patients to have a hip replacement without needing to stay overnight in the centre.

REFERRAL AND ASSESSMENT:
1. **Referral** – Patients are referred to the orthopaedic centre by their GP or another healthcare provider.
2. **Initial assessment** – Upon referral, patients undergo an initial assessment to evaluate their condition and determine the appropriate treatment plan.

PRE-OPERATIVE PREPARATION:
1. **Pre-assessment clinic** – Patients visit the pre-assessment clinic, where they undergo various tests and evaluations (e.g. blood tests, ECG, X-rays) to ensure they are fit for surgery.
2. **Consultation** – Patients meet with the surgical team to discuss the procedure, potential risks and benefits, and post-operative care.

SURGERY:
1. **Admission** – Patients are admitted to the centre on the day of their surgery.
2. **Procedure** – The surgery (typically a hip or knee replacement) is performed by a specialized orthopaedic surgeon.

POST-OPERATIVE CARE:
1. **Recovery** – After surgery, patients are monitored in the recovery ward before being transferred to a regular ward.
2. **Rehabilitation** – Physical therapy and rehabilitation begin shortly after surgery to aid recovery and improve mobility.

DISCHARGE AND FOLLOW-UP:
1. **Discharge** – Patients are discharged once they meet specific recovery criteria, typically within a few days of surgery.
2. **Follow-up** – Follow-up appointments are scheduled to monitor the patient's recovery, address any concerns and ensure the success of the surgery.

FIGURE 12
Patient pathway at the orthopaedic centre

BRING WHOLE WORK TEAMS TO LIFE IN YOUR ORGANIZATION

How can we practically incorporate this ability to 'adapt and improve' into our organizations? The fundamental principle is that we need to organize around whole work teams that have a purposeful activity and outcomes that they can plan, do and improve. In practical terms, this can be achieved through the use of a number of different team mechanisms. Four of the most popular are summarized in *Table 6* with examples from different companies and the impacts they have delivered.

WHOLE TEAM IMPROVEMENT APPROACH	EXAMPLE BUSINESS USAGE	APPLICATION AREA	KEY IMPROVEMENTS/ RESULTS
Kaizen	Toyota	Car assembly process	Reduced assembly time, increased productivity, reduced waste[41]
Lean Six Sigma	General Electric	Jet engine manufacturing	30% reduction in defects, substantial cost savings[42]
Agile development	Spotify	Music streaming platform	Quick adaptation to user feedback, continuous improvement of user experience[43]
Quality circles	Tata Steel	Energy consumption in blast furnace operations	Significant reduction in energy use, lower operational costs, smaller environmental footprint[44]

TABLE 6
Example team mechanisms that can drive improvement

These team mechanisms are drawn from wider approaches to improvement, but are underpinned by the principle of whole work teams that are able to plan their work, deliver it, review the effectiveness and improve the way that it is done. Each of the approaches is appropriate in different circumstances, as explained in the following paragraphs.

Kaizen, a Japanese philosophy meaning 'continuous improvement,' is widely used in manufacturing and business environments. Kaizen teams focus on small, incremental changes to improve efficiency, reduce waste and enhance quality. These teams often include employees from various levels of the organization who collaborate to identify areas for improvement, implement changes and monitor the results. These teams have the advantage of diversity of skills and insight, which they use to bring about their innovations, although a potential downside is that they may be disbanded or reformed after delivering improvements.[45]

Toyota is well known for its implementation of kaizen. At Toyota, kaizen teams involve employees at all levels working together to improve manufacturing processes. One notable example is when a kaizen team at Toyota's plant in Georgetown, Kentucky, improved the assembly process by rearranging tools and modifying the workflow. This resulted in a significant reduction in the time required to assemble a car, leading to increased productivity and reduced waste.[46]

Lean Six Sigma combines lean manufacturing principles with Six Sigma methodologies to enhance process efficiency and eliminate defects. These teams typically consist of trained professionals, including 'green belts' and 'black belts,' who work on specific projects aimed at reducing variability, improving quality and optimizing processes. The teams use data-driven approaches to identify problems and implement sustainable solutions. Lean Six Sigma provides a powerful toolkit for delivering ongoing, incremental change to measurable processes although it can emphasize efficiency ('doing things right') rather than effectiveness ('doing the right thing').

General Electric is a strong proponent of Six Sigma and has successfully used it to improve its processes. A Lean Six Sigma team at GE's aviation division worked on reducing defects in jet engine manufacturing. By using Six Sigma tools and lean principles, the team was able to identify the root causes of defects, streamline processes and reduce variation. This resulted in a 30% reduction in defects and substantial cost savings.[47]

Agile development teams are used in business, particularly in software development and product management. They are formed to enhance adaptability and responsiveness to customer needs. These teams follow agile methodologies, such as Scrum or Kanban, to work in iterative cycles, deliver incremental improvements and quickly adapt to changing requirements. Agile teams are cross-functional, comprising members with diverse skills who collaborate closely to achieve common goals. Agile approaches are increasingly popular outside their 'home ground' of software development because they allow for early delivery of what is termed by agile software developers as a 'Minimum Viable Product' (e.g. an online banking application) and then ongoing enhancement so users get more and more features over time.[48]

Spotify, the music streaming service, is noted for extensively employing agile methodologies. Spotify's agile development teams, known as squads, work on different aspects of the platform, such as user interface, recommendations and payment systems. These squads operate in iterative cycles, constantly testing and releasing new features. This approach allows Spotify to quickly adapt to user feedback and market changes, continuously improving the user experience.[49]

Quality circles are small groups of employees who regularly meet to discuss and solve workplace problems. Originating in Japan, these circles focus on enhancing product quality, productivity and employee morale. Members of quality circles voluntarily participate, bringing their unique perspectives and expertise to identify issues, propose solutions and implement changes. These teams empower employees to take ownership of process improvements and foster a culture of continuous development. Quality circles are particularly popular in manufacturing settings, where teams can be physically together and sit down regularly (e.g. daily) to address issues and find solutions quickly.[50]

Tata Steel in India has implemented quality circles to enhance its operational efficiency. In one instance, a quality circle focused on reducing the energy consumption in the company's blast furnace operations. By analysing data, brainstorming solutions and implementing changes, the team was able to achieve a significant reduction in energy use, leading to lower operational costs and a smaller environmental footprint.[51]

THE POWER OF ADAPTATION AND IMPROVEMENT

As this chapter has set out, our bodies are built around the ability to adapt, improve and develop over time. This is achieved by different parts of our bodies adapting and changing without recourse to central analysis (by our brains). This allows our bodies to quickly adapt to new circumstances, from changes in temperature to the need to develop survival skills. Our organizations need this same ability to adapt, such as by moving away from traditional bureaucracy with a 'command-and-control' centre.

Building around whole work teams, whether these are lean teams, agile squads or other structures, offers the possibility of organizational agility and resilience. As discussed, there need to be various conditions in place to make organizations successful. These conditions include breaking work down into purpose-driven teams (with aligned measures) that can plan, do and improve the work they are tasked with. The right leadership and team skills need to be in place at the right 'human scale.' There are many options, but embracing one of the team mechanisms discussed in this chapter is non-negotiable for organizational survival.

KEY LEARNING POINTS

- Our bodies are made up of many parts and systems that are able to adapt and improve without reference to our brains, allowing rapid, ongoing adaptation (an example is our muscles, which develop via a process called hypertrophy).

- For organizations to embrace such adaptation, they need to be organized around the concept of whole work teams, which have a well-defined purpose and aligned measures, and are able to plan, do and improve their work.

- Whole work teams need the right environment to be successful, including the right leadership and team skills, at the right 'human scale.'

- Whole work teams may be structured differently depending on the type of underlying work, the degree of change and innovation required, and the improvements needed – examples of whole work teams include kaizen teams, Lean Six Sigma teams, agile development teams and quality circles.

- Many organizations have seen dramatic improvements through embracing this ability to adapt and improve, including Toyota (through kaizen), General Electric (through Lean Six Sigma), Spotify (through agile development) and Tata Steel (through quality circles).

APPLICATION EXERCISE

Consider a team in your organization where you've identified a need for improvement. Consider the following questions while applying the six characteristics of whole work teams shown in *Figure 11*:

1. What is the purpose and significant output of the group? How would we measure it?

2. What people (skills and roles) do we need in the group to achieve the purpose?

3. What development and tools do the team need to help them innovate and improve?

4. How can the team leader and organization ensure the conditions for continuous improvement?

CHAPTER 7
COORDINATION OVER HIERARCHY

**Living Organization Characteristic 5:
Integrated and Balanced**

- Living organizations need access to external and internal data (stimuli) so they know how and when to adapt.

MICROMANAGEMENT FROM THE TOP

I turned up at the station of a medium-sized town in the North of England to start my project with a defence engineering company. As I looked down the high street of the town, the backdrop was dominated by the sight of two large hangars where the company designed, constructed and maintained complex military vehicles. They had been making vehicles for the UK armed forces for nearly 100 years and the town had been shaped by this core industry. Local schools and colleges were a pipeline of talent for the future, with many schoolchildren following their parents into work at the facility.

I was leading a project to help the site attract and grow the workforce from around 3,000 people to around 7,000 people as they were ramping up for a new class of vehicles for the future defence of the nation. The site included extensive infrastructure, such as specialized production lines, testing facilities and hangars to ensure that each vehicle met rigorous standards for performance and reliability. The workforce was substantial and highly specialized, including engineers, designers, project managers and support staff.

We started the work in earnest, engaging senior leaders, specialized engineers, skilled trade staff, professional support staff and union leaders. Despite the sophistication of the work and the expertise of the staff, it became clear that the organization was far less sophisticated. Team leaders complained that they often had to go up five levels of management to get a decision on a small area of design. Union leaders said they chose to bypass middle management because they just got in the way and ultimately members of the executive would give them a clear decision. Micromanagement of work was rife, with the executive getting involved in plans for the next quarter rather than planning for the future against their pipeline of ten or more years of work. At the shop floor level, I talked to a group of specialist welders who had worked at the plant for over 15 years and were doing work that few in the world could undertake, yet they had not been placed in any position of authority or given a status commensurate with their ability. Despite them having deep experience, their voices were largely ignored. Progression was generally obtained by moving sideways, out of their areas of expertise into broad, general management.

My team and I saw a massive opportunity to empower people within whole work teams (as discussed in the previous chapter). We also saw that these teams could work together in wider, coordinated groups to take on design and build tasks for parts of the vehicles, without reference to senior people. However, we were going to need to achieve clarity around who decided what, reduce the levels of management to what was really required and find ways to help people get coordinated.

THE BODY DOES IT BETTER:
COORDINATION OVER HIERARCHY

The previous story illustrates the fact that organizations tend towards either chaotic (disordered) or bureaucratic structures that don't support responsive and agile coordination of activities. However, our bodies have sophisticated systems that coordinate our activities, without defaulting to the brain (the body's equivalent of the executive!) for every decision. How does our body achieve this and what can we learn from it?

It surprised me to learn that our bodies have 11 coordinating systems. These systems all work together and depend on each other to function. They are shown in *Table 7* on the next page.

BODY SYSTEM	PURPOSE
Skeletal	Provides structure, support and protection for the body; facilitates movement; produces blood cells; stores minerals
Muscular	Allows for movement, stability and posture; generates heat
Lymphatic	Defends against infection and disease; transports lymph, a fluid containing white blood cells, throughout the body
Respiratory	Enables breathing; exchanges oxygen and carbon dioxide between the air and blood
Digestive	Breaks down food into nutrients; absorbs nutrients; eliminates waste
Nervous	Controls and coordinates body activities; processes sensory information; enables thought and memory
Endocrine	Produces and secretes hormones; regulates bodily processes such as growth, metabolism and reproduction
Cardiovascular	Transports blood, nutrients, gases and wastes throughout the body; maintains body temperature and fluid balance
Urinary	Removes waste products from the blood; regulates blood volume and pressure; controls levels of electrolytes and metabolites
Reproductive	Produces sex cells (sperm and eggs); facilitates reproduction; supports the development of offspring
Integumentary	Protects the body from environmental damage; regulates temperature; provides sensory information

TABLE 7
The 11 coordinating systems of the body

Table 7 illustrates some powerful characteristics of our bodies. It is useful for us to learn from them as we develop and shape teams and organizations:

- Different elements of a healthy body are **delegated to different body systems** (groups of organs and cells) in the body rather than a single hierarchy of control.
- The connective systems are then **coordinated at different levels** with **higher-level systems**, such as the nervous and cardiovascular systems, **coordinating lower-level** systems (such as digestive).
- Various forms of communication, such as enzymes and nerve signals, achieve coordination; this ensures that **multiple sets of information are incorporated into decision-making and control.**

The sophistication of this coordination is illustrated by looking at the digestive system. The digestive system is a complex network of organs that work together to break down food into nutrients, which the body uses for energy, growth and cell repair. The process begins in the mouth, where chewing and saliva (containing the enzyme amylase) start the breakdown of carbohydrates. The food then travels down the oesophagus to the stomach, where gastric juices, rich in acid and the enzyme pepsin, further digest proteins. The acidic environment in the stomach not only helps to break down food but also kills harmful bacteria. From the stomach, the partially digested food moves into the small intestine, where the process of breaking down fats begins.

The control of pH (acid versus alkali) and the action of enzymes are crucial in the digestive process. Different sections of the digestive tract have different pH levels, optimized for the specific enzymes that work there. For instance, the stomach's low pH (around 2) is ideal for initial digestion but would block most of the enzymes that are active in the small intestine, where the pH is closer to neutral (around 7). Enzymes (biological catalysts) are highly specific and function best at particular pH levels and temperatures. The precise regulation of pH ensures that enzymes function efficiently, allowing the digestive system to effectively break down food into its constituent nutrients, which can then be absorbed into the bloodstream and transported to cells throughout the body.

This sophisticated coordination of digestive activity allows us to enjoy a good dinner! It also keeps our bodies healthy and balanced.

CONNECTING TEAMS TOGETHER TO ACHIEVE PURPOSE:
THE VALUE CHAIN

The previous section described how individual organs and cells work together in different levels of sub-systems (such as the digestive, nervous and muscular systems) to achieve results. Clusters of different types of cells work together to perform specific functions. They then link together into sub-systems (as discussed in the previous section). In turn, the various sub-systems work together to create a healthy human being.

In organizations, we need to understand the right 'clusters of cells' that work together to satisfy the overall customer need. We do this through a concept known as the 'value chain.' The value chain categorizes the generic value-adding activities of an organization. It is how we bring together the activity steps that an organization needs to undertake to go from capturing a customer need (through marketing and sales) to delivering effective services (to satisfy customer needs). Alongside this core value chain, there are management and support activities that play a coordinating role. As a specific example, *Figure 13* shows the value chain for a scientific services company that I once worked with. The activity steps take us through the process from capturing the customer's need to deliver services that satisfy that need in a commercially advantageous manner.

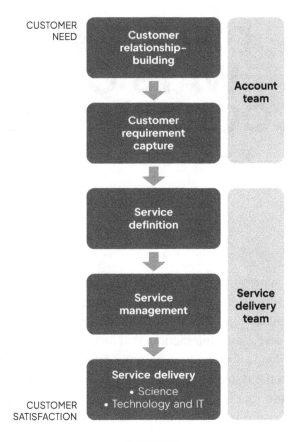

FIGURE 13
Value chain for sales and service management
in a scientific services company

This value chain concept helps us to cluster and coordinate teams together to achieve a part (and, ultimately, the whole) of a process that serves customers. The scientific firm had an account team dedicated to building relationships and capturing requirements for customers (e.g. a chemicals firm). The account team would pass the requirements to a services management team to define, manage and oversee delivery of these services. So, the value chain was delivered (at this level) for a particular account through an account team and a service management team. At a higher level, there was a need to coordinate and manage this overall sales and delivery process across all of the firm's customers as part of delivering the organizational purpose. We will explore how these levels of coordination work later in this chapter.

DIFFERENT WAYS OF COORDINATING

How can we learn from and replicate the body's sophisticated way of coordinating activity in our teams and organizations? We have learned some important lessons from the body about how coordination happens and also the levels and interaction that occur between coordination mechanisms. Next, we'll look at how we might replicate some of the learning about the systems and mechanisms of coordination. I've chosen five mechanisms that have been used effectively in organizations I have worked with or seen at close quarters. They are summarized in *Figure 14*.

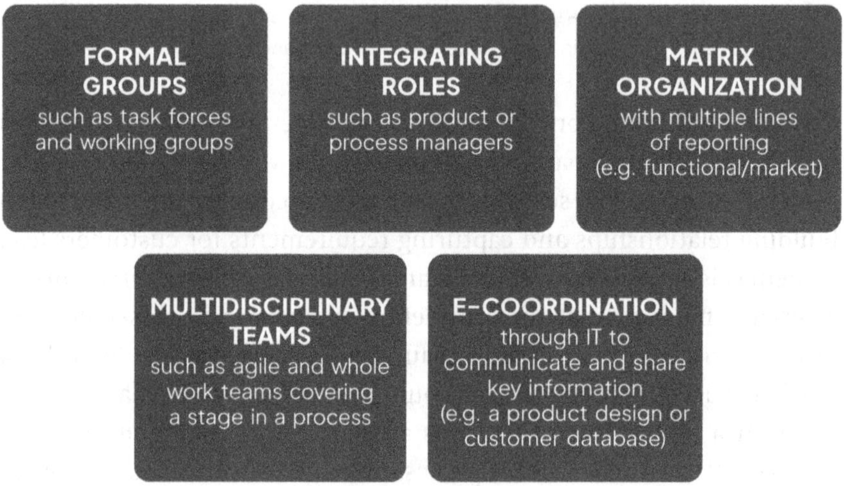

FORMAL GROUPS
such as task forces and working groups

INTEGRATING ROLES
such as product or process managers

MATRIX ORGANIZATION
with multiple lines of reporting (e.g. functional/market)

MULTIDISCIPLINARY TEAMS
such as agile and whole work teams covering a stage in a process

E-COORDINATION
through IT to communicate and share key information (e.g. a product design or customer database)

FIGURE 14
Five types of coordinating mechanisms in organizations

Formal groups would include working groups formed to deliver a particular outcome. They are typically temporary, with a limited life span. For instance, in a consultancy I worked for, we created a task force that looked at the long-term plan for the workforce, taking into account the firm's business strategy and the challenges of attracting the right kind of people. It delivered a five-year view and was then disbanded.

More permanent ways of creating integration adjust the underlying structure of the organization permanently. A strong movement in recent years has been towards creating product-based organizations with product managers. This is an example of an **integrating role**. For instance, Microsoft appoints an overall Microsoft Word product manager responsible for the evolution, development and market success of this product.

Another way of achieving a similar result is the **matrix organization**, with the concept of dual reporting. If we extend the example of Microsoft, they could choose for software engineers to report both to a product team (e.g. Microsoft Word) and to a functional team (e.g. software engineering) that is responsible for the professional development of its software engineers. A key ingredient in the success of this coordination approach is clarity around what responsibilities each of the dimensions of the matrix are responsible for managing. The software engineers on the Microsoft Word team may be measured in terms of productivity (coding goals completed) by the product manager and also on their development of new practices that benefit the broader software engineering community, measured by metrics defined by the software engineering function.

Currently, a popular way of creating coordination is through agile teams, which are an example of 'whole' (see previous chapter) **multidisciplinary teams**. A whole, multidisciplinary team is responsible for an entire stage of a task and for continuing to develop the way in which that task is undertaken. When working with a police force, my team and I created multidisciplinary teams that investigated and dealt with specific types of crime, such as serious and organized crime and child protection. The teams would have appropriate make-ups to deal with the whole issue. For instance, the child protection team would draw in social services to ensure protection orders could be put in place for vulnerable children. We will look at an example of agile teams in the next section.

Finally, the advance of technology has enabled more sophisticated ways of coordinating teams – **e-coordination**. In *Chapter 1*, we encountered the Dutch healthcare organization Buurtzorg. They use technology to efficiently coordinate their decentralized and self-managing teams. The primary tool Buurtzorg employs is a custom-designed digital platform called Buurtzorg Web. This intranet-based system facilitates communication, scheduling and administrative tasks, allowing nurses to manage their caseloads and collaborate effectively without the need for traditional management hierarchies. Buurtzorg Web includes functionalities for patient record management, care planning and real-time data-sharing, ensuring that all team members have access to up-to-date information and can coordinate care seamlessly.[52]

We can draw some lessons on how we might choose the right forms of coordination for our organization from looking back at how the body coordinates activity. Some key questions to ask are:

1. **What types of work/activities do we want to coordinate around?**
   What are the main steps in the value chain that we could coordinate around? In the body, we see the digestive system as a single coordinated area of activity. If we are primarily based around products, then we should consider a product-based organization with groups led by product managers, potentially in agile teams. If we need to keep a careful eye on aligning to both customers and a set of services, then a matrix organization may be better.

2. **Is the coordination temporary or permanent?**
   If the work is temporary, then a task force or working group is likely to be better. In the body, we see permanent systems (such as digestion) as well as local responses to an event (e.g. to healing a cut).

3. **Does the coordination mechanism link to other parts of the organization appropriately?**
   Coordination mechanisms should link together – both hierarchical and across the organization. In the body, coordination mechanisms

form a complex hierarchy with the nervous and cardiovascular systems sitting at a higher level than areas such as digestion. So, we should decide on appropriate levels of connecting mechanisms so that local empowerment and central coordination can coexist. The mechanisms should fit with the overall design choices, such as whether we want a matrix or product organization.

DIGITAL REAL ESTATE:
COORDINATION THROUGH AGILE TEAMS

The client had an ambitious agenda. They want to create a digital company for real estate transactions for buyers and sellers of homes across several European countries. They had the advantage that they had already bought smaller firms operating in individual markets. One of these firms had a powerful feature to allow customers to look at an area or road in a city and see how expensive and attractive it was. The user could display this information as a heatmap (see *Figure 15*). Other features had been developed by some of the smaller firms, including links to legal services, so the whole transaction could be managed online.

Chapter 7   Coordination over hierarchy

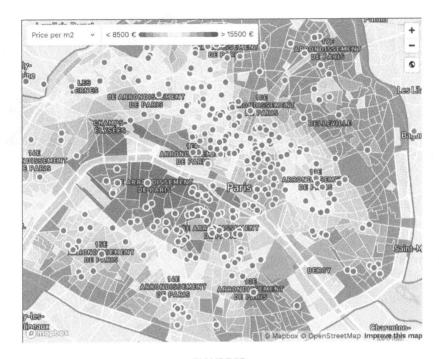

FIGURE 15
Heatmap of house prices in a European city

The ambition and need were clear. Several disparate firms needed to be brought together, bringing the best of their services into a single digital platform. Various structures in the firms differed, although all had strong software teams that could develop the online platform. The challenge was to organize and coordinate their activities so that an integrated, best-in-class service could be delivered across all the European countries. How could this level of integration be achieved while giving a distinct national, customer-centric flavour to the digital real estate service in each country?

At the centre of this firm, we agreed, was the product – an online digital offer that linked together house buyers, house sellers, estate agents and other professionals (finance and legal). The integration of the product led to the decision to adopt a product-based organization with product owners. To ensure customer-centricity, the products were aligned to the customers and the customer journey, as shown in *Figure 16* on the next page.

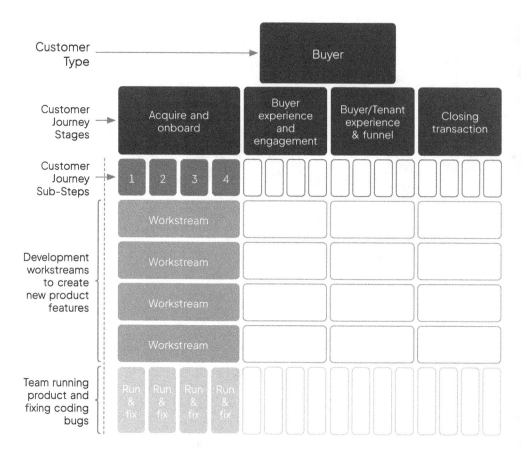

FIGURE 16
Product teams aligned to the buyer (seeker) journey

The buyer (seeker) journey involved four broad stages: acquiring a new buyer, engaging the buyer to seek out potential properties, funnelling down choices to a potential purchase and closing the deal. This was reflected in a product organization scheme with an overall product owner responsible for every stage of the customer journey, with one product owner per customer type (buyers, sellers and estate agents; *Figure 16* shows just the buyer journey). The buyer product owner was given responsibility for revenue from the house buyers, which incentivized them to focus on the features of the digital product that most attracted, engaged and drove sales of properties. Each product journey team was then led by a sub-product owner who was responsible for that stage of the journey. So, for example, the Acquire and Onboard Team was responsible for defining how they would use social media to attract potential customers to the real estate site and then onboard them, getting them to log in, create an account and share the desired qualities of the property they were looking for.

The teams needed to be whole, with the capacity to develop the online site and also ensure it performed well with the customers. So, multidisciplinary, whole, agile teams were required, each led by the product (or sub-product) owner. Typical roles on a team would include product owner, squad lead, user experience designer, DevOps (code developers), a data architect, and a data and analytics engineer. Each team had members who specialized in the customer experience and in customers' requirements for the product experience. This included roles such as research manager, user interface designer and front-end developer. These roles worked closely with those involved in designing the product experience, such as the developers (DevOps, backend developer and information security engineer) and those involved in the data analysis that underpinned the real estate transactions.

To get the team members working together effectively as a group, there needed to be a regular cadence to the meeting of this 'squad' through a rhythm of sprints (typically two- to three-week development stages). These included initial planning, daily 'stand-up' meetings, a closeout and a review (retrospective). This enabled both close collaboration and regular outputs that improved the customer experience. New features could be released to customers quickly – in a few weeks – rather than waiting for months using traditional functional teams. Through the user of a higher-level structure of product owners for each of the three customer types (buyer, seller and estate agent), coordination was maintained across the firm and across the customer experience.

COORDINATING AT DIFFERENT LEVELS:
THE CONCEPT OF WORK LEVELS

The case study illustrates the importance of two elements: collaboration within teams and coordination at different levels (right up to the top level – the customer experience and delivery). In the agile organization, there were different levels of team related to the overall product (real estate trading platform), customer specific product (e.g. for a home buyer) and sub-product (e.g. customer acquisition). In a living organization, it is vital that both horizontal and vertical integration exist. In typical bureaucratic (functional) organizations, there is little or no horizontal integration, requiring many decisions to go up a long chain of vertical command, with all the ensuing frustration and slow decision-making.

Fortunately, there is some useful theory that we can draw on and practically apply to help us with this vertical integration. It enables us to minimize the number of vertical levels and flatten the structure, leading to flexible, responsive and agile responses from the organization. From the late 1970s, Elliott Jaques pulled together work on the 'theory of requisite organization,' which includes a framework for organizational structure, management and HR, emphasizing the alignment of work complexity with employees' capabilities.[53] A central element of this theory is the concept of 'work levels,' which classifies work into up to seven distinct levels based on complexity and timespan. The concept is shown in *Figure 17*.

LEVEL OF WORK	TIMESPAN	THEME	TYPICAL ROLES	PRIMARY FOCUS
7	More than 20 years	Shaping context	CEOs of global enterprises	Shaping the future
6	10–20 years	Environmental screening	CEOs of international organizations	Shaping the future
5	5–10 years	Strategic direction	CEOs of national organizations	
4	2–5 years	Strategic development	Divisional and functional heads	Planning for the future
3	1–2 years	Systematic coordination	Unit and departmental heads	
2	3 months to 1 year	Diagnostic judgement	Front-line managers and specialists	Managing the present
1	1 day to 3 months	Routines and practical judgement	Front-line and clerical staff	

Diagram based on work of Professor Elliott Jacques

FIGURE 17
Elliott Jaques' work levels concept of
a maximum of seven levels in an organization

The theory of requisite organization suggests that the levels in an organization should have distinctly different planning timespans and decision-making focuses. This ensures that the time frames and complexity of decision-making are kept separate. Jaques argued that even the largest global organizations should not have more than seven levels.

Throughout my career, the theory of requisite organization has helped me to make sense of structures and simplify them to ensure people can work effectively and efficiently together. When I was working with a well-known global logistics firm, the theory allowed us to plot the current and future levels of work. Parcels were processed on a *daily* basis by sorting staff (work level 1) in teams of up to 20 people, with a supervisor on a packing line (work level 2) who coordinated the *monthly* rotas. The supervisors were overseen by depot managers (work level 3), who ensured that the *annual* forecast and operational plan were converted into monthly forecasts and staffing requirements that the supervisors could then plan and manage staff to execute. We ensured that the clarity of these levels of planning and governance persisted high up, including among regional managers (work level 4), zone leads (work level 5) and global staff (work level 6). Work level 7 was not needed.

Sometimes these levels aren't as clear as they were in this logistics firm, so it may be necessary to use deeper work- and job-evaluation methods. However, the thinking and approach typically bring a reduction in unnecessary levels and the resulting frustration of slow decision-making.

CHILDFUND INTERNATIONAL SPONSORSHIP:
INTEGRATION AND THE 'MISSING MIDDLE'

My team and I worked with ChildFund, a global child welfare and sponsorship charity whose mission is to "help deprived, excluded and vulnerable children have the capacity to improve their lives and the opportunity to become young adults, parents and leaders who bring lasting and positive change in their communities."[54] This powerful mission has led ChildFund to help more than 36 million deprived and vulnerable children and family members in its more than 70-year history.[55] ChildFund's strong sense of purpose has driven the building of an extensive network of devolved and empowered local organizations and communities of people across 23 sponsorship countries on three continents – Africa, the Americas and Asia.[56]

ChildFund is devolved because it is geographically spread out and culturally varied. Local determination is central to its development aims. A dilemma of success lies in the tension between the strong, centrally held founding mission and the growth in the quantity and diversity of ChildFund's local development organizations and communities. Each region goes through a learning process about the most effective way to make real, sustainable differences to the lives of children and families. These insights need to be shared and potentially transferred and built into more strategic approaches to development and sponsorship so that lessons don't need to be regularly relearned. For instance, individual countries have innovated in the way that sponsorship activities (e.g. sponsored children writing letters and receiving physical check-ups) are integrated into development work (e.g. through sporting and educational days where letters are written as part of educational activities). This type of learning needs to be shared quickly and effectively.

Without somewhere to locate this coordination activity, a 'missing middle' appears in this type of organization between the executive team (who own the purpose and mission) and the operational communities (who deliver the development outcomes).[57] This leads to inefficiency (through duplication of activity at different levels and lack of sharing of best practice), donor disappointment (through a variable experience of the organization) and falling short of the stated mission.

At ChildFund, the concept of work levels helped us to understand which work levels were adding to delivery of the mission of the organization and which were unnecessary and leading to overlapping responsibilities. In particular, it allowed us to see how the missing middle layer of integration between executive direction and operational delivery could be bridged. The central work of the organization was building a financially and emotionally supportive relationship between communities of children and sponsors (people and organizations). This involved three key elements:

- **Child engagement** – supporting families and building a community around the child to support their physical, emotional and cognitive needs so they could grow into a healthy adult through provision of education, nutrition and wellbeing enhancements.
- **Sponsor engagement** – sharing the nature of the need and how they could make a difference through supporting a systematic and inclusive process of child and community development.
- **Relationship-building** – building an informed and equal relationship between sponsors, children and their communities to ensure a sustainable and growing relationship.

These elements of the sponsorship relationship needed to be supported at each level in the organization. We identified four work levels: executive direction, cross-organizational sponsorship, regional sponsorship management and in-country sponsorship operations. *Figure 18* shows the work levels as well as where each activity happened in the ChildFund organization. A new role and level were created around a vice president of sponsorship to ensure systematic nurturing of the sponsorship relationship over the long term.

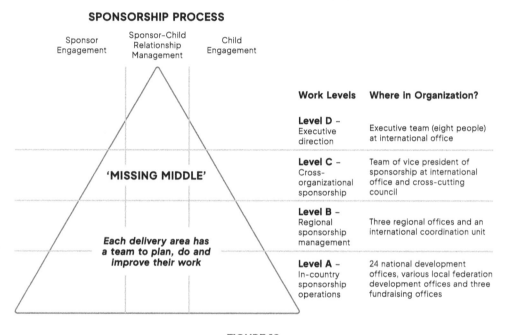

FIGURE 18
Creating a missing level to coordinate sponsorship activity

The clarity gained from the concept of work levels allowed staff to be much clearer about the roles of teams and leaders. Each level had a clear time span for decision-making, ensuring that micromanagement and duplication of work were eliminated. This also ensured that the missing strategic direction for sponsorship had clear ownership and a team that looked at the long-term development of relationships. This led to the development of internet-based communications and secure online message boards giving updates on child and community development. Approved photos could be posted, and deeper relationships and support ensued.

This case study illustrates how an organization can remain living and dynamic if it has strong integration both horizontally and vertically.

Work levels and the theory of requisite organization can help us understand which vertical work levels are essential (and which are not needed) and vertical integration. The concept of the value chain and the various forms of cross-cutting coordination bring clarity to how we achieve horizontal integration.

KEY LEARNING POINTS

- Organizations tend towards either chaotic or bureaucratic structures that don't support responsive and agile coordination of activities.

- Our bodies do it better through two types of mechanism:
  - Cross-cutting coordination – through different body systems, such as the nervous system.
  - Different levels of coordination – from the cellular level to sub-systems (e.g. the digestive system) to higher level systems (e.g. nervous system) to the whole body (often under the direction of the brain).

- Horizontal (cross-cutting) coordination is achieved by linking together the stages of customer delivery, known as the value chain.

- Cross-cutting coordination can be achieved in several ways, depending on the overall organizational form chosen, including:
    › Formal groups – such as a customer task force or working group.
    › Integrating roles – such as product or process managers.
    › Matrix organization – including multiple dimensions of coordination (such as market sector and service area).
    › Multidisciplinary teams – where agile or whole work teams come together around stages in a workflow or value chain.
    › E-coordination – enabling information flows and rapid contracting between different teams.
    › Different reporting/vertical levels in an organization should all add value to the achievement of the overall purpose; in general, organizations have too many levels that have been added for reasons of grading and status rather than to align with work levels reflecting different time frames and complexities of decision-making.

APPLICATION EXERCISE

Consider your current organization's structure and the different levels of reporting. Compare them to the work levels introduced in *Figure 17* to help you determine whether you have too many levels in your organization (or your part of it).

Discuss your findings with a colleague.

CHAPTER 8
CONTINUOUS DEVELOPMENT AND GROWTH

**Living Organization Characteristic 6:
Lifelong Growth (Part 1)**

- Adaptation and evolution are central to humans' survival and development.
- Living organizations should adapt and evolve as they grow (and have mechanisms and attitudes to enable this).

OFF SHE GOES...

She was 11 months old. She burst away from the settee and tottered across the room to my wife. Hannah's first completely unaided walk. Like all parents, we were excited and delighted. Like we had with so many of her physical achievements, we'd (literally) watched the steps towards this moment. Early on she was laid on her stomach on a soft mat, allowing her to kick, roll over and crawl – this is all about building strength. As her muscles strengthened, she began to sit up, initially supported by furniture or a helping hand from one of us. This stage builds further strength and coordination.

She then moved into her 'cruising' stage. We had a long sofa along one side of the room that she could hold on to, which allowed her to take some side steps. This allowed her to practise balance and weight-shifting. She developed a fondness for a trolley with bricks in it that allowed her to stand and move as part of cruising. Gently, she tried releasing herself from the edge of the sofa or trolley and standing up on her own. This independent standing allowed her to develop her balance before that magic moment with the first steps.

A few weeks later, we wondered what the fuss had been about as she became confident and proficient in walking – coordinating her movements, improving her balance and walking longer distances. Now that she is a teenager it seems an age ago, but the same pattern of learning and growth has been repeated as she has learned to drive a car.

WHAT DOES THIS TEACH US ABOUT HUMAN GROWTH?

Hannah's story teaches us four things:

- Growth is a learning process – there are new skills at each stage of the journey.
- Failure is involved – falling over is part of the process.
- Lots of effort, resilience and determination are required – the whole process involves going again and again.
- The process also needs aim, purpose and inspiration – there is an aim and ultimate purpose to this learning that allows children to move on to the next stage of development and achievement.

Yet, contrast this with our organizations. So often, people are measured against targets before they have learned a job or skill. Failure is punished so people stick to what they already know. In a world that needs organizations to innovate to serve clients and customers, we have blame cultures that stimulate the caution and avoidance of risk-taking.

Carol Dweck formalized and gave depth to this insight in her research on fixed and growth mindsets (see *Table 8*). She began researching the topic in the 1970s, initially focusing on students' responses to failure. Her research group at Stanford University conducted studies revealing how beliefs about intelligence influence resilience, motivation and achievement. They identified two key mindsets: fixed, where abilities are seen as innate, and growth, where abilities can develop through effort. Through experiments and studies, Dweck's team demonstrated that a growth mindset fosters greater persistence and adaptability. The growth mindset has now become common parlance in both business and education and has influenced approaches to learning and people development.[58]

FIXED MINDSET	GROWTH MINDSET
Belief: Your qualities are fixed and can't be changed.	**Belief**: Your qualities can be developed and changed through effort.
Definition of success: Being mistake free, smart or 'right.'	**Definition of success**: Growth and improvement.
CONTRASTING FOCUSES OF FIXED VERSUS GROWTH MINDSETS	
Focus on validation: Focus on how others think of you. Seek validation to appear smart and successful.	**Focus on learning**: Focus on stretching yourself and seek opportunities to learn and improve.
Seek certainty: Thrive in the comfort zone where success is certain. Driven by the desire to prove yourself.	**Seek challenges**: Thrive with challenges and learning experiences. Driven by the desire to push your boundaries.
Pre-judge potential: Believe success is due to innate talent/abilities. Inflate your current abilities to feed your ego.	**Seek ongoing improvement**: Believe any area can be improved. See your abilities objectively and thereby know what and how to improve.
Crack under failure: Label yourself a failure and give up. Place blame or find excuses to protect your image.	**Grow from failure**: See mistakes as problems to overcome. Identify shortfalls and find new ways to succeed.
Reluctant to put in extra effort: Associate effort with inferior ability. Silently worry that your best effort isn't enough.	**Accept effort as key to success**: Know effort is crucial regardless of talent. Believe in working towards mastery.
Threatened by others' success: Feel good when comparing yourself to those who are worse off. Ignore criticism or evidence that others are better.	**Learn from others' success**: Seek inspiration from others who are better. Welcome feedback and constructive criticism.

TABLE 8
Summary of growth versus fixed mindsets (based on the work of Carol Dweck)[59]

When we view organizations as machines, we see people as components that either 'work' or 'fail.' This reflects the fixed mindset, which is based on a core belief that intelligence and talents are fixed. Underpinning the growth mindset is a belief that intelligence and abilities can be developed through effort, learning and perseverance. Scientists have discovered how 'plastic' our brains are,[60] with the ability to reshape and reform based on different stimuli. The evidence shows everyone can develop their capacity rather than being trapped by their current cognitive capacity. They also show that the early years of a child's life are critical for brain development, with up to 1 million new neural connections forming every second. Without adequate stimulation, these connections may not develop properly, potentially leading to deficits in cognitive, language and social skills.[61] This is termed 'sensory deprivation.' Do our organizations also suffer from such 'sensory deprivation' when leaders foster blame cultures and fail to offer developmental experiences?

Science shows us that there is a great opportunity here. If we can cultivate a growth mindset then employees will develop much greater persistence and resilience, which lead to higher performance and better-quality outputs. Language is a key factor. When we praise effort over innate ability and encourage experimentation then employees grow, become more engaged, and develop new avenues for their own personal growth and the growth of the organization. At a real estate firm, one new employee said to me that her career had been fundamentally changed when her manager had said "You're allowed to make mistakes, you know!" after she had worked in a blame culture for the previous five years.

This belief in organization, team and human growth is applicable across academia, sports, arts and business. It also releases the power of diversity, improves inclusion, creates stronger engagement, drives innovation and improves retention.

HOW DO WE LEARN AS INDIVIDUALS?

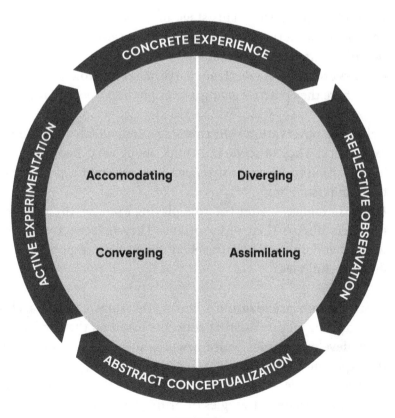

FIGURE 19
Kolb's learning cycle[62]

David Kolb's learning cycle, as presented in his book *Experiential Learning*,[63] is a model of learning that emphasizes the process through which people learn through experience. The cycle, shown in *Figure 19*, consists of four stages: concrete experience, reflective observation, abstract conceptualization and active experimentation. The theory emphasizes that individuals only learn through active (concrete) experiences of the world and then develop theories and concepts about how life and the world works, which they test and refine through active experimentation and application. It is useful to examine how the learning cycle works in more detail, with examples taken from business:

1. **Concrete experience** – This stage involves having a new experience or encountering a new situation. It can also be a reinterpretation of existing experiences.
   Business example – A sales team participates in a role-playing exercise where they practise giving a sales pitch to a potential client.

2. **Reflective observation** – In this stage, individuals reflect on the experience. They observe and think about what happened, paying attention to any inconsistencies between their experience and their understanding.
   Business example – After the role-playing exercise, the sales team members discuss their observations. They reflect on what went well, what didn't and how the client might have responded to different techniques.

3. **Abstract conceptualization** – During this stage, individuals form new ideas or modify existing concepts based on their reflections. They develop theories or frameworks to help them understand the experience better.
   Business example – The sales team analyses their reflections and comes up with new strategies or principles for making a successful sales pitch. They might develop a new sales approach or refine their existing techniques based on what they learned from the role-play.

4. **Active experimentation** – In this final stage, individuals apply their new ideas or theories to the world around them. This stage involves testing the new strategies in practice to see if they improve the outcome.
   Business example – The sales team implements their new strategies in actual sales meetings with clients. They experiment with different techniques they developed during the abstract conceptualization stage to see which ones yield the best results.

The learning cycle draws out five important factors in personal and team learning:

- Learning involves ongoing application, experimentation and observation of the real world.
- People need time to draw out learning, theories and frameworks alongside this experience.
- People need access to existing theory and knowledge that they can build on and develop.
- Failure is an essential and inevitable part of learning.
- People have different preferences and strengths across the learning cycle, so learning is best done as a team to draw on different strengths.

LEARNING ACROSS A MULTINATIONAL OIL AND GAS FIRM

So, what does this look like in practice and how can it be harnessed to improve individual, team and organizational results?

A large multinational oil and gas company that I worked with drills into rock formations both on land and under the sea. This is a very expensive business, with well-drilling typically costing around $1 million per day. However, the efficiency and effectiveness of this process can be significantly improved – in other words, oil can be discovered more quickly – through rapid learning about how to drill through different rock formations. In practice, making improvements in the capture and application of this knowledge delivers at least a 10% performance improvement and around a 10% cost reduction. Throughout a drilling programme, this equates to an excess of $100 million of savings.

In this company, the Exploration and Production group set up a large community supported through a Well Engineering and Performance Forum. The forum allowed international cooperation on technical and business issues related to drilling. Over time, frequently asked questions and lessons learned were captured to be turned into operating procedures, training and standard approaches.

A performance analysis of this learning was undertaken across two major areas that had been drilled between 1997 and 2005. The results are shown diagrammatically in *Figure 20*. One area employed 'fast learning,' where a community of 1,250 exploration and drilling staff posed around 2,000 questions and offered around 10,000 answers via the forum. The learning resulted in over 10% cost savings and the drilling speed got faster and faster over time. In contrast, in the area where no learning was applied, no improvements were made over time.

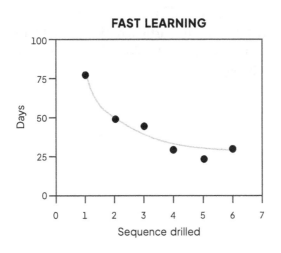

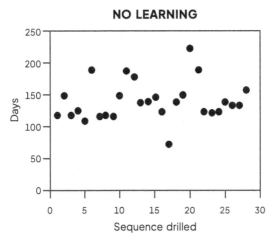

FIGURE 20
Well-drilling performance improvements achieved through a learning forum versus with no learning

This is an example of a continuous cycle of learning in an organization. It had significant positive impacts for the development of people and knowledge, and ultimately for the financial results. My team and I were inspired to take this further and see how it could be applied to other areas of the business. In particular, we worked with the Global Digital Communications and Technology division, which will be covered later in this chapter.

HOW CAN AN ORGANIZATION CONTINUOUSLY DEVELOP?

Drawing on the earlier insights from Kolb's theory of learning, we went on to look at the work of Ikujiro Nonaka and Hirotaka Takeuchi, who had gone a step further to look at how a cycle of learning can operate at the team, division and organization levels.[64] The core concepts of their knowledge-creating company concept are illustrated in *Figure 21*.

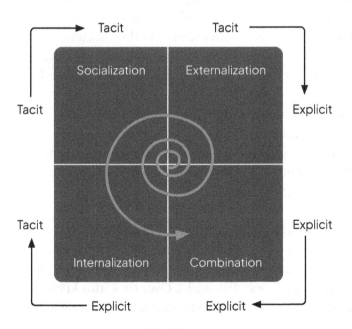

FIGURE 21
Ikujiro Nonaka and Hirotaka Takeuchi's concept of a knowledge-creating company

The focus of their research was Japanese companies and how the dynamics of knowledge creation, learning and innovation work. The model centres on the interaction between two types of knowledge:

- **Tacit knowledge** – This is 'in people's heads' and is personal, based on experience and hard to set out formally. For instance, writing music requires a form of tacit knowledge.
- **Explicit knowledge** – This is formal, codified knowledge, such as standard company procedures expressed in a flowchart of operations.

The dynamic process of knowledge creation, therefore, has four parts.

1. **Socialization (sharing tacit knowledge)** – For example, in a software development team, a junior developer learns debugging techniques through pair programming with a senior developer. This hands-on experience transfers tacit knowledge directly through shared work experiences.

2. **Externalization (converting tacit knowledge to explicit knowledge)** – For example, a marketing team conducts brainstorming sessions to gather creative ideas and then documents these ideas in a company marketing strategy. Here, the abstract ideas (tacit knowledge) are turned into a written plan (explicit knowledge).

3. **Combination (systematizing explicit knowledge)** – For example, a multinational corporation gathers best practices from different branches worldwide and compiles them into a comprehensive operations manual. This process combines diverse, explicit knowledge into a unified system.

4. **Internalization (converting explicit knowledge back to tacit knowledge)** – For example, after attending a workshop on new project management tools, employees start applying the learned techniques in their daily tasks. Over time, this knowledge becomes second nature, so it is transformed into tacit knowledge.

In this theory, the emphasis is on the growth and development of knowledge between tacit knowledge, typically gained informally through day-to-day experience, and explicit knowledge, typically resulting from formal attempts to codify knowledge so it can be written down and taught in a more traditional sense. The process parallels many of the concepts of Kolb's experiential learning cycle.

APPLYING THE KNOWLEDGE-CREATING COMPANY CONCEPT

Drawing on our earlier learning from the Exploration and Production community study and also on Nonaka and Takeuchi's concept of the knowledge-creating company, my team and I were able to build an approach, environment and enablers for continuous growth and development across the Global Digital Communications and Technology (DCT) function of the multinational oil and gas company. We drew together examples of the four areas of learning and knowledge development and tailored them to the environment of this multinational.

We created a cross-company IT mentoring scheme between a global IT firm, a global automotive firm's IT function, and this oil and gas company. This was a form of tacit-to-tacit learning (socialization), involving taking the experience of other IT professionals and enabling less experienced staff to learn from their experience and share issues and dilemmas that they could solve together. We developed global communities of practice around topics such as IT application management and IT project management. This involved regular conferences with speakers (captured on video for later reference) and experienced professionals to capture particular areas of learning (e.g. project benefit management) so they could be distilled into written-down good practices. These were examples of tacit-to-explicit learning (externalization).

Figure 22 shows a summary of the eight major ways in which we enabled learning across the global DCT function. It was important that we covered all four modes of learning and knowledge creation, to create a virtuous learning cycle and ultimately allow the company to meet its aspiration to be a learning organization. The mechanisms worked at multiple levels (individual, team, organization and in some cases cross-organization) to form a 'spiral of learning.' For instance, mentoring acted at the level of one-to-one individual learning whereas the expertise search mechanism allowed anyone globally to find the relevant expert group, team or individual.

FIGURE 22
Practical mechanisms of growth across knowledge creation cycles

WHAT DID THESE VARIOUS LEARNING APPROACHES LOOK LIKE IN PRACTICE?

Table 9 on the following pages provides a summary of what these different elements of the overall learning process for the global DCT function included. We drew on external examples of successful practice to minimize the amount of testing time required to deliver results. However, every context is different and each of the mechanisms took time to get right. It was important that the various mechanisms fed into each other (e.g. mentoring towards a professional accreditation and aligned training) and that there was a single point of overall governance for the DCT's various areas (such as IT security, IT architecture, project management and applications management).

MECHANISM	EXAMPLES
Mentoring and coaching (Tacit to tacit)	• Put in place a basic framework and administration for the mentoring and coaching of IT professionals (under the central IT development team). • Identified senior-level mentors and coaches (internal and from external companies) and less experienced staff to be mentored on a regular basis (identification carried out by IT domains, e.g. IT architecture).
Expertise search (Tacit to tacit)	• Provided an electronic AI tool that identified experts on topics relevant to IT within the business, creating searchable profiles and using keyword analysis. • Created a globally searchable company LinkedIn-style profile system. • Enabled employees to enhance their profiles to show more of their experience so they could help with queries and move into interesting work areas. • Allowed individuals to highlight areas of development and interest on their profiles.
Communities of practice (Tacit to explicit)	• Set up or facilitated a small number of groups associated with key topics in certain domains and cross-domains. • Put in place performance measures, a participation schedule, facilitator training, technology support and links to advisory groups.
Electronic forums (Tacit to explicit)	• Provided a Q&A forum with topics arranged by domain subject area. • Set up central moderation and encouraged active involvement of domain teams.

MECHANISM	EXAMPLES
Centres of expertise (Explicit to explicit)	• Created a small central team to manage knowledge bases and a regular programme of training and events. • Published best-practice process descriptions and associated documentation. • Provided training and other resources in key tools for specific domains (e.g. project management tools). • Managed accreditations and certifications of practitioners.
Linking knowledge into business processes (Tacit to tacit and tacit to explicit)	• Identified the key process in each domain (e.g. incident management, project lifecycle stage management, service level management), linking the work of communities of practice into improvements of these processes globally. • Created a knowledge-capture and knowledge-sharing process (i.e. knowledge plan, peer review(s), retrospectives and after-action reviews) linked to documentation storage (e.g. best-practice documentation).
Training and development (Explicit to tacit)	• Implemented a mixture of on-the-job, online and classroom development in core topics.
Accreditation and certification schemes (Explicit to tacit)	• Linked accreditation and certification to the main technology domains (e.g. project management, IT architecture).

TABLE 9
Overview of learning mechanisms employed in the multinational oil and gas company's Global Digital Communications and Technology function

WHAT WERE THE CONDITIONS FOR THIS GROWTH?

We started this chapter with the story of my daughter learning to walk, noting that all learning involves stages of growth, failure and development and the right environment. Organizations need the right environment to grow, just like dutiful parents provide a supportive environment for their children to grow.

As part of the work with the global DCT function, we studied the ingredients that had made many of the external examples of learning successful – we termed this a 'peer review' – and made sure we built these lessons into our approach around each of the learning mechanisms introduced previously. We initially piloted each of the mechanisms in an individual IT domain (e.g. application management) so we could prove and refine the concept. At the end of each pilot, we ran a 'retrospective' that covered a number of questions to develop learnings around how to scale the concept and ensure it was sufficiently robust to deliver for the global function.

This work and experimentation formed the essence of my master's dissertation on organizational development.[65] In my research, I found that five conditions needed to be in place to make a mechanism and approach sustainable. They are summarized in *Figure 23*.

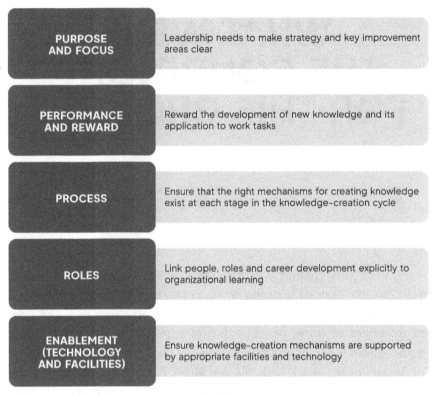

FIGURE 23
Essential organizational conditions for learning

Humans are motivated to learn when they see a clear **purpose** and application for their learning. This was made clear for the staff in the DCT function by linking their learning back to their area of IT. To reinforce this motivation, specific objectives were both publicly and financially **rewarded**, with these objectives related to raising the expertise of the communities staff were part of (e.g. running project management training courses for colleagues). People also need the 'how' – a **process** by which they can learn and apply the learning. In this light, the company project delivery process was explicit about how knowledge and learning were applied at the start (peer review), during (retrospective reviews of tasks) and after action (capture of lessons at end of project). For this to happen, people needed to be clear on their **roles** in learning and **enabled with appropriate technology** (online forums and knowledge-capture software).

KEY LEARNING POINTS

- Adaptation and evolution are central to humans' survival and development.

- A growth (rather than fixed) mindset is essential among employees for individuals and teams to grow (as outlined by Carol Dweck).

- Individuals grow by moving through an experiential learning cycle – applying ideas out in the real world (concrete experience), understanding what worked and what didn't (reflective observation), building better cognitive theories of the world (abstract conceptualization) and then moving on to new approaches (active experimentation).

- Similarly, living organizations should adapt and evolve as they grow.

- In a similar way to an individual undertaking experiential learning, living organizations move through a spiral, multi-level learning process that involves shifting knowledge between explicit (documented and recorded) and implicit (held in people's minds) forms.

- For organizations to grow, this spiral of learning and growth needs to be supported.

- There are five environmental factors that need to be in place for an organization to enable continuous growth and learning:
  › Purpose and focus
  › Performance and reward
  › Process
  › Roles
  › Enablement (technology and facilities)

APPLICATION EXERCISE

Consider a division or function in your own organization (or the whole organization if you are in a small organization). Turn your attention to how good you consider your organization (or the division you have chosen) to be at learning and developing over time, moving in close harmony with the market and embracing the ingenuity of its people.

Firstly, consider the following questions:

1. What is the main purpose of your organization or division?

2. How is success measured? How successful has your organization or division been over the past few years (or choose an alternative sensible time period in light of the speed of business in your sector)?

3. What improvements and innovations have been made over the past few years?

4. Is your organization or division good at learning and development?
   a. What is good?
   b. Where does it fall down?

Secondly, look back at the eight mechanisms for the oil and gas company (see *Figure 22*) and consider what your organization's or division's equivalents are. Where are the gaps? What mechanisms could you introduce to enable improvement and innovation in your organization or division?

Consider plotting them in a similar way to *Figure 22*.

Lastly, consider how your organization or division measures up against the five critical conditions introduced in *Figure 23*. Score the current status using either a scale or simple yes/no answers. You can then identify what is needed to create the conditions for growth and innovation in your organization or division.

Build a simple plan to pilot and iteratively improve how well your organization or division learns and develops in sync with your market and customers.

CHAPTER 9

GROWTH STAGES IN ORGANIZATIONS

**Living Organization Characteristic 6:
Lifelong Growth (Part 2)**

- Living organizations, like people, move through 'life stages' of development, characterized by different structures and ways of being.

GROWING UP

In the previous chapter, I related a segment of my daughter's early development as she learned to walk at around a year old. Hannah's development has been marked by hundreds of different learning experiences – some physical, like learning to walk; some cognitive, like learning maths; and some emotional or social, like forming friendship groups. Organizations, too, experience hundreds of daily, weekly and annual examples of learning and improvement.

However, humans have a higher level of development. My early years (ages 0–5) were marked by learning to walk, speak and developing deep attachments to my parents. I began to understand how the world worked and laid the foundations for my future growth. The middle years of my childhood (6–12 years) were spent at three different junior schools and included a move from York to Warwickshire, near the birthplace of William Shakespeare. My development shifted to more formal learning at school, where I developed a strong interest in maths and engineering with a mild obsession with Lego alongside a passion for biking with friends that has remained throughout my life. I built friendships beyond the home with children from my village and school. I also started to develop my own ideas about life – specifically right, wrong and fairness.

Like most people, I found that moving into the teenage years (ages 12–18) brought significant change, both positive and at many times confusing and challenging. At around age 15 I started my first serious relationship with a girl, who helped me a lot in exploring who I was and what I was committed to. I was fortunate to have a clear sense of what work and study I wanted to do (engineering and business) but slower to become comfortable with my own emotions (like many boys!). My early adulthood (ages 19–30) saw me leave home to study at university and break out into a career in technology and then consulting. I joined various clubs, including a squash club, and became actively involved in the community through a church. My career began to develop as I started to manage teams and shifted from technology into people development and organizational consulting. I seemed to have endless energy for socializing and sports.

Life has shifted considerably in my middle age (age 30 to the present). I met my wife in my early thirties. With this came a multitude of changes including the birth of our two daughters, a house move (to accommodate them), pushing on in my consulting career (partly to earn the money to support a family) and a sharpened sense of the purpose of life and what's important.

There are still future challenges awaiting me: moving into old age (60 years and beyond) and retiring from full-time paid work. I have always had a love of bikes, and although this passion is as deep as ever, I have purchased my first electric mountain bike as I begin to adjust to the decline from my physical peak in my thirties.

While no two people's lives follow exactly the same pattern, you will undoubtedly recognize these stages in your own life, albeit in very different circumstances. As we reflect on these stages of life, there are a number of lessons that we can draw out:

- **Life develops in recognizable stages of growth and transition** – such as the significant transition into teenagerhood and adolescence around the age of 12 or 13.
- **The focus of development in each stage is considerably different** – for example, on leaving home, our focus shifts to creating a life independent of our parents and developing new social relationships around us.
- **Changes involve emotional, cognitive and physical shifts** – our underlying purpose and identity take time to surface and become clear to us (and others).
- **What worked in one stage doesn't necessarily help us in the next stage** – for example, we learn a lot physically early on in our lives, but it doesn't prepare us for the process of self-discovery in our teenage years.

TIME FOR OUR ORGANIZATIONS TO 'GROW UP'

Many academics and commentators, notably Larry Greiner in his famous *Harvard Business Review* article "Evolution and Revolution as Organizations Grow,"[66] have noted the way that organizations parallel human development. His article presents a model of the growth stages of organizations, which are characterized by periods of evolution (steady growth and development) and revolution (crisis-driven change).

Greiner outlines five key phases of growth: creativity, direction, delegation, coordination and collaboration. Each phase begins with a period of evolutionary growth, but as the organization matures, it encounters a crisis that necessitates a revolutionary shift to the next phase. For example, after the initial creative phase, organizations face a leadership crisis, requiring more structured direction. Similarly, each subsequent phase presents challenges – such as autonomy, control or excessive bureaucracy – that must be resolved through significant changes in management practices. Greiner's model emphasizes that organizational growth is not linear but cyclical, with each phase bringing new opportunities and challenges that require adaptation and transformation.

I have often heard people in organizations talk about their own firm as 'needing to grow up,' frustrated with its problems and inadequacies. My own boss once referred to the consultancy we were working at as an 'awkward teenager' because it was full of potential but didn't really know how to harness that potential in a consistent and coherent manner. In webinars and business school sessions, I find that executives can quickly identify a 'life stage' that their organization is in. This enables us to sharpen our focus on the issues that we face, recognizing that we need to distinguish between ongoing improvement (evolution) and these changes of organizational life stage (revolution).

GROWTH AND LIFE CRISES IN PROFESSIONAL SERVICES FIRMS

Like people, every organization is different, and each one has stages of development that we can begin to recognize. I have been deeply involved with many different types of professional services firms, including three major legal firms, two large accounting firms, numerous consulting firms, four asset management firms, and a number of marketing agencies and consultancies. Over a period of 30 years, I have seen the same issues occur across these apparently very different firms when they reach a particular scale and level of complexity. I saw growth stunted in at least three of the consultancy firms because they either failed to recognize the transition they needed to make or were not prepared for the upheaval of dealing with it.

In the early stages when a firm is relatively small – perhaps a consultancy started by a couple of ex-partners from a larger organization – there is an explosion of creativity as the initial group work with clients they know around problems they have experience of, often bringing new and emerging ideas. Creativity is king! However, there comes a point, perhaps when the firm is reaching higher double figures (50 or more staff), when people and activity require greater coordination and leadership direction. Creativity has turned into confusion.

Based on my experience and research, I have distilled five stages of development, summarized in *Figure 24* on the next page. Each has an associated growth characteristic, and a crisis point. These stages are typical and archetypal. In practice, some firms choose to remain at a particular stage of development because they do not wish to grow beyond a certain size or because elements of the environment restrict them from growing (e.g. lack of capital investment available to fund the next stage of development). Even within professional services, the sub-sectors face sector-specific challenges, such as specific regulatory changes or requirements for funding that will further shape the exact nature of these stages. However, the stages provide a powerful guide for recognizing the maturity and growth of a professional services firm.

		Growth through	Crisis
Start-up/ new entrant		Creativity	Leadership and coordination
Managed firm	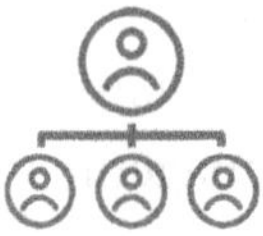	Direction	Autonomy
Distributed firm		Delegation	Control
Coordinated firm	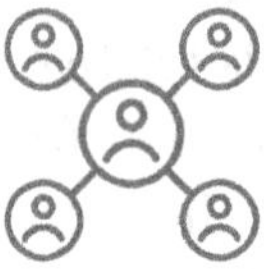	Coordination	Red tape
Collaborative firm		Collaboration	Continued innovation?

FIGURE 24
Typical growth stages in a professional services firm

The stages provide some important lessons and insights that can help leaders and investors avoid firms failing or losing out to the competition. These lessons include:

- **Founders need to know when to leave or release power** – Would Google have grown to its large scale without Larry Page and Sergey Brin allowing Eric Schmidt to come on board as CEO and shape and manage the firm?
- **Each stage of growth sows the seeds of crisis for the next stage** – As management provides more direction, individual and team autonomy may be reduced, resulting in less innovation and responsiveness to customer needs.
- **Different business and operating models are needed for different stages** – Early on, a location-based model is typically effective. But, as a firm gets larger, it becomes increasingly important to collaborate across locations around services or larger accounts.
- **New technology and organizational forms can help to resolve the tension between coordination and empowerment** – New technologies and data-sharing can empower more networked organizational forms that enable innovation and agility at scale.

MAKING THE SHIFT SUCCESSFULLY:
AN ACCOUNTING FIRM

The European market for accounting services is fiercely competitive. Every trading organization needs to use both auditing services (to check and verify accounts) and accounting services (to manage the financial trading activity of the firm). The European market for audit and accounting services had a total estimated value of €225.6 billion in 2024, with audit worth around €61 billion and accounting services worth €164.6 billion.[67] Alongside the 'Big 4' accounting firms (Deloitte, EY, KPMG and PwC), there has been a rise of smaller and mid-size firms that have grown from niche and specialist organizations into larger firms.

This case study is based on an accounting and audit firm that I advised in 2023. It had grown to have over 1,500 employees across around 15 European offices. Some of the growth had occurred through evolution. A single office was opened in a major city like London and then further offices were opened across the UK as business was gained in different locations. The firm's early European expansion was fuelled by a number of acquisitions of small European firms, often serving particular niches such as trusts, estates and advertising companies. Each office was led by a group of partners, with each one typically looking after two to five clients that they had developed over time with associates undertaking the detailed work. The work done by each office always included core audit and accounting, but the mix of other work depended on the clients served.

At this point in its growth, after over 20 years of growth as a distributed, location-focused business, the firm was showing significant signs of crisis. For example:

- **Shortages of skills in certain locations** – Some offices lacked the expertise to do work in important client areas, such as corporate tax, due to lack of local talent. In contrast, there was a surplus of this expertise in other areas of the business.
- **Loss of work due to lack of awareness of what the firm was capable of doing** – Often clients would approach the firm asking for a specialist service and were told the firm couldn't offer it, even though other offices had the relevant experts.
- **Lack of staff mobility and opportunity** – The office-based culture limited opportunities for staff to move across offices and upwards in their career trajectory. Career progression was largely based on a partner taking someone under their wing and helping the person work with their clients.

According to the model of growth shown in *Figure 24*, we see a firm that is at a crisis point between being a distributed firm and a coordinated firm. The leadership recognized that there was a need to move from 'offices as islands' to coordinating services across offices. Some services, such as mergers and acquisitions (which the firm specialized in), became coordinated at national level, though still marketed through local offices. This meant the firm could share these skills between offices, sell more of this work to clients (through greater awareness of firm capability), and offer staff the ability to move nationally and internationally.

Some of the critical elements of this shift involved:
- Moving from a location-based organization to a matrix of offices and services.
- Adopting a new governance structure with some services led nationally and some led locally (if they were only relevant to a particular region or group of clients).
- Career structures and skills management systems that enabled associates to identify their skills in particular service areas so they could be more mobile and visible and progress on the basis of their ability.
- Resource management across the firm, allowing people to work across offices rather than just be tied to a particular office, partner or client group.

KEY LEARNING POINTS

- Living organizations, like people, move through 'life stages' of development, characterized by different structures and ways of being – these are periods of steady growth and times of upheaval where there are fundamental shifts.

- Organizations need to learn to recognize these stages and adapt their processes, structures, rewards, focus and technology accordingly.

APPLICATION EXERCISE

Think about where your organization is in its development (or you may wish to choose another organization that you have worked with). Consider the following questions:

- What image or analogy would you use for the stage of growth that the organization is in (e.g. 'start-up toddler,' 'awkward teenager' or 'learned elder')?

- Is the organization growing successfully? What is working well?

- Are there signs of crisis or underlying issues?

- What phase of development are you at (refer back to *Figure 24*)?

- What is the nature of the challenge or crisis the organization is facing?

- What action should you (or the leadership) consider as a result to successfully move the organization into the next stage of growth?

CHAPTER 10
LIVING IN AN ECOSYSTEM

> **Living Organization Characteristic 7:**
> **Networked**
>
> - People are not islands but communities.
> - Living organizations need to understand their core capabilities and where they must cooperate and form partnerships to achieve their highest purpose.
> - Networks enable a 'higher purpose' to be achieved.

COMMAND AND CONTROL IN AN AUTOMOTIVE FIRM

FAVI is an automotive firm based in Hallencourt in northern France.[68] It was founded in 1957 and has built a strong reputation in the automotive industry, particularly for its gearbox forks, which are used by major car manufacturers across Europe, and its high-quality brass and aluminium die-cast components.

The company had a traditional command-and-control structure. By the early 1980s, this had led to an atmosphere in which employees were disengaged, innovation was stifled, and the company was slow to respond to market change. For instance, if a worker noticed a defect in a product or a process issue, they were expected to report it to their immediate supervisor, who would then escalate it through the management chain – a time-consuming and thankless task. Innovation was also stifled. As one employee put it:

> Change was something to be feared. If you wanted to keep your job, you did things exactly as you were told. New ideas were not welcome.

This directly affected the service that customers received as employees were made to focus on doing their job efficiently against strict targets, taking the focus off the customer. As another employee put it:

> We didn't know who our customers were, or what they wanted. Our job was just to make parts, nothing more.

In 1983, a turning point was reached in a rather unconventional fashion. The founder, Max Rousseau, decided it was time to change things. He invited Jean-François Zobrist, one of his senior team, into his office. He led him out to his helicopter, which was already waiting. As Zobrist recounted:

> He took the seat next to the pilot and I sat in the back. I was relaxed, not thinking about much and mostly enjoying the landscape. An hour later we arrived above FAVI in Picardy and landed on the field just in front of the factory. Dominique (the CEO at that time) had heard the noise and arrived immediately next the helicopter. Max told him: "Gather the staff."
>
> When all the staff arrived, around 100 employees, Max said: "Dominique did an excellent job, and he wants to leave. It is his right, so I let him go." Then Max turned to me, pointed at me and told the crowd: "This is his successor!". Without any other comment he went back to his helicopter and left immediately.[69]

It was a moment of revelation and transformation As Zobrist went on:

> I knew that we had entire freedom from Max Rousseau, so I started dreaming. I was dreaming of a company where the worker would become the operator. A place where operators would be able to organize themselves, adjust machines themselves and auto-control themselves.[70]

This was followed by a period of reflection and solidification of ideas around how to realize this dream. The answer was based on an ecosystem of mini-factories rather than traditional command-and-control structures. It also required a fundamental shift in the organization's culture, leadership and approach to business.

The starting point was engendering a culture of trust and decentralizing power. Zobrist believed that people would do their best when they were trusted, so time clocks and traditional performance reviews were dismantled. Pivotal to customer focus and empowerment was the creation of 'mini-factories,' where teams were organized around specific customer segments. This allowed teams to take full ownership of their relationships with customers, leading to increased accountability and quality. For example, a mini-factory team noticed a recurring issue with a product part that had already been delivered to a client. Rather than waiting for a directive from management, the team halted production, fixed the issue and informed the client. The client was impressed and gave FAVI more business long term.

The environment and enablers changed. Central planning was removed and replaced with team-based decision-making. For instance, teams could decide who should join and leave rather than this being determined by a central HR department. Zobrist believed that those closest to the work and the customers were best positioned to make decisions, rather than senior managers. He also extended freedom and responsibility to teams, allowing them to manage their own work hours rather than 'clock watch.' The message was clear: "We trust you to do what's right." Ensuring employees are connected to the purpose of their work – both for their families and for FAVI – has been central to motivation. As Zobrist has said, *"People don't come to work for FAVI; they come to work for themselves, their families, and their customers."*

Ultimately the firm has emerged stronger and much more resilient and agile than its competitors. Many struggled through the 2008 financial crisis but FAVI's growth continued due to its rapid adaptation to changing market conditions. After the implementation of Zobrist's management changes, FAVI experienced a significant productivity boost, reportedly of 50%. FAVI has also reported a dramatic reduction in employee turnover, which has dropped to nearly zero.

WHAT HAS CHANGED?

Why is there a need to change the structures and ways of working that served us in the post-war period? It is because the environment of business has fundamentally changed. The post-war period was marked by a period of stability, with strong government-led planning that lent itself to the command-and-control structures of bureaucracy. In the UK, the government embarked on major house-building and infrastructure projects. The core of the modern National Health Service was developed. Though the scale increased, and organizations became more complicated, the underlying environment still allowed for longer-term plans, budgets and activity.

The world has become complex and unpredictable. The term VUCA (volatile, uncertain, complex and ambiguous) was coined to encompass this based on research I undertook in 2022; six major trends have coincided to drive this change. They are summarized in *Figure 25*. In the external world, there has been **significant political and social volatility**, including wars in the Middle East and Eastern Europe alongside the COVID-19 global pandemic. Partially linked to this, there have been periods of both raw materials and labour **scarcity**. The rise of technology has helped to fuel two associated trends. The first is a growing **customer-centricity**, including the concept of 'micro-segments,' where clients can buy unique products. For instance, Rolls-Royce boasts that it now never makes the same car twice as its cars are so personalized.[71] Secondly, **business models are being reinvented** with the emergence of platform businesses such as Airbnb and Uber. However, this is competing with a growing recognition that a world based purely on profit is unsustainable, and a renewed focus on **sustainability** across people, planet *and* profit is emerging. Finally, post-pandemic, people are recognizing that **work is changing** permanently, and new hybrid ways of working will emerge.

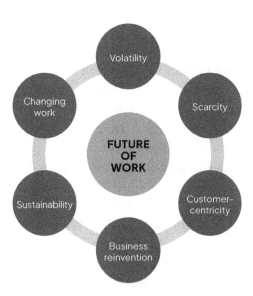

MEGATREND	WHAT IT ENCOMPASSES
Volatility Think • VUCA world, agility and risk mitigation	• Political disorder • Global power shifts • Pandemic to endemic
Scarcity Think • War for talent and cost pressures	• Talent scarcity and the Great Resignation • Raw materials scarcity
Customer-centricity Think • Individuality and micro-segments	• Diversity • Demographic shifts • Urbanization • Social disparity
Business reinvention Think • Uber, Industry 4.0, Big Data, AI	• Digital transformation • Ecosystems • Platform businesses • Industry mash-ups
Sustainability Think • People, planet and profit	• Climate change and the environment • Social and societal value
Changing work Think • Tech-enabled, hybrid workers	• Hybrid work • Dynamic skills development • Augmented human capabilities • Decentralized work

FIGURE 25
Six major trends driving the future of work and organizations

A fundamental part of this shift is the reinvention of businesses and organizations, which have shifted from hierarchies (focused on control) to networks (focused on empowerment and innovation). Initially there was an emergence of teams within hierarchies but organizations like FAVI are providing a blueprint for 'teams of teams.' This is because they need to reflect the complexity of their environment. Ross Ashby puts this succinctly, saying, "If a system is to be stable, the number of states of its control mechanism must be greater than or equal to the number of states being controlled."[72] Martin Reeves also comments on how the inside of our organizations must mirror the complexity of our wider business world and environment: "We may think about ecosystems as an external appendage for the firm. But we can't really have a complex two-sided marketplace or main business model involving thousands of other enterprises, unless we change the inside of the firm, too."[73]

HOW DO LIVING ECOSYSTEMS DEAL WITH THIS COMPLEXITY?

We can again see that living systems deal admirably with this complexity. In the heart of a forest, life thrives as a living ecosystem where every element is interconnected. The trees, providing shelter and food, rely on animals for seed dispersal and pollination, illustrating the ecosystem's interconnectedness. The forest is a tapestry of life, with its diversity contributing to its resilience, just as a coral reef's varied species make it adaptable to change.

Sunlight drives the energy flow, nourishing plants that sustain herbivores and predators, creating a balanced chain of life. Beneath the soil, recycling and sustainability take place as decomposers return nutrients from fallen leaves to the earth, ensuring ongoing fertility.

The forest is also a story of adaptation and evolution. Species continually adjust, like cacti storing water in deserts, showcasing nature's ability to meet challenges. Despite constant change, the forest maintains a dynamic equilibrium. After a wildfire, life slowly returns, demonstrating the ecosystem's resilience and balance.

Over time, the forest evolves, transforming barren land into a thriving ecosystem after events like volcanic eruptions. This ongoing evolution reflects the gradual, inevitable march of nature.

HOW CAN ORGANIZATIONS REFLECT THE INHERENT WISDOM OF NATURE?

In *Chapter 2* we were introduced to Haier, the Chinese multinational consumer electronics and home appliances company known for its innovative products and customer-centric business model. It has attempted to emulate the features of an ecosystem in the core elements of the organization. We can see parallels between Haier's principles and many of the insights used to reorganize FAVI, as described earlier in this chapter. Though it takes time, these firms show that this shift is both possible and beneficial. So, what are some of the key features of an organization modelled on an ecosystem'

'MICRO-FACTORIES' AND 'MICRO-ENTERPRISES' ENABLE TEAM-BASED EMPOWERMENT

With FAVI, we were introduced to 'mini-factories,' where teams were organized around specific customer segments. This allowed teams to take full ownership of their relationships with customers, while having full decision-making power over themselves and their processes. Haier has a similar concept of a network of micro-enterprises (MEs) that operate like independent start-ups, with decision-making autonomy. Relationships between MEs are governed by dynamic contracts that outline mutual goals, performance metrics and profit-sharing mechanisms. These contracts ensure alignment with customer needs while fostering collaboration across different MEs. Many MEs will be internal but some MEs might be external small firms providing a specific service.

Consider how, in your own organization, a team might be able to oversee a whole unit of production (like the drug production line in *Chapter 6*).

AN ECOSYSTEM OR NETWORK NEEDS THE RIGHT CONDITIONS TO ENABLE DEVELOPMENT

We are used to seeing nature flourishing as we walk around beautifully tended gardens and natural landscapes. However, when drought comes, ecosystems can be devastated. The same is true of ecosystems – the right conditions need to exist. These conditions are physical in the natural world whereas they are cultural in the organizational world. Three conditions are as follows:

- **Empowering leadership** is required for the team-based empowerment of MEs. The purpose of the leader shifts from directing operations to ensuring teams are effective at sourcing and using the breadth of capability within the team. Leaders need to think of themselves as gardeners, leading by example, to cultivate a new environment.
- **Shared purpose** needs to be infused across the network – through leadership, incentives and close connections with clients. Without empowering leadership and shared purpose, ecosystems can become introspective and ME teams can flounder, although an ME can 'die' (go bankrupt), and the network will adapt. This involves transparency of information across the network, lateral connections, and clarity on the ultimate purpose and outcomes.
- An **entrepreneurial mindset** is required to make any network flourish. At FAVI, the employees had to shift from 'being told' to 'taking control.' This involved creating new innovations, bringing people with the right skills on board, and selling the benefits to customers and other parts of the network. For employees who have been told to 'do and not think,' there may need to be a significant development effort to shift this culture.

DYNAMIC AND ADAPTIVE STRUCTURES ENABLE COORDINATION AND RESPONSIVENESS TO THE ENVIRONMENT

While MEs bring the innovation, empowerment and ownership to core teams, these teams need ways of coordinating activity and collaborating. In network organizations, there are typically a few types of structures and processes that enable this in a dynamic and fluid manner:

- **Ecosystem micro-communities (EMCs)** – MEs are organized into EMCs, which share common goals and customer segments, and deliver an important outcome or service. For instance, an EMC might be responsible for the production of a fridge, linking together MEs that deliver parts of this production (e.g. wiring of electrics).
- **Shared service platforms** – Like any business, a network business needs support services (such as HR, finance, IT and legal). However, unlike in other businesses, these may be decomposed into MEs or formed into EMCs (and named shared service platforms).
- **Industry platforms** – Network organizations aim to devolve decision-making to the ME teams. So how can focus and strategic direction be set without top-down, command-and-control structures? When you recognize that networks work more like markets (internal and external), decision-making can be influenced by providing investment targeted on sectors and products that are seen to have growth potential. This is done through industry platforms, which act as sources of investment capital (like an external private equity firm might) focused on, for instance, providing investment in the electric automotive sector. Industry platforms are a lean supporting structure that coordinates investments and local strategic decisions.

It is interesting to reflect on how the network organization reflects our forest ecosystem discussed earlier, with diverse elements coming together to create growth. It is not centrally controlled but based on the interaction of different species, seasons and sources.

FURTHER EXAMPLES

FAVI is an example of this ecosystem approach in a manufacturing setting, but what can it and does it look like in other settings?

ZAPPOS

Zappos,[74] an online retailer known for its exceptional customer service and wide selection of shoes, clothing and accessories, adopted Holacracy in 2013 to transform itself into a self-managing organization.[75] This decentralized management system replaced traditional hierarchy with a network of roles and circles, empowering employees to take on multiple roles, fostering agility and innovation. The goal was to create an adaptive organizational ecosystem that encouraged entrepreneurial thinking. While the transition faced challenges, including confusion and some employee departures, Holacracy reinforced Zappos' focus on autonomy, flexibility and purpose. Ultimately, it contributed to Zappos' commitment to delivering outstanding customer service and maintaining a dynamic, responsive organization.

THE HOXBY COLLECTIVE

Another interesting example is the Hoxby Collective. This is a social enterprise community of freelance professionals that assemble and disband as needed, depending on project requirements. Since 2015 Hoxby has promoted the WorkStyle philosophy, which allows individuals to choose when, where and how they work, and this fosters diversity and inclusivity. The ecosystem thrives on shared values, trust and a common goal of delivering high-quality work, supported by digital tools that facilitate collaboration, communication and project management.

The collective has no offices, employees or fixed working hours. It operates with over 500 team members in 43 countries, delivering creative communications and employee experience projects for companies such as AIA, AWS, Merck and Unilever. Hoxby aims to create a happier, more fulfilled society by promoting work without bias. I spoke to one of the founders, Alex Hirst, who co-authored a bestselling book on the subject of WorkStyle[76] and is now actively working to build inclusivity in work environments through collaborations with UK charities and employers.

Hoxby has a decentralized structure based around self-managed teams, allowing freelancers to work whenever and wherever they are most productive. Teams are assembled based on project requirements, drawing from a global network of freelance specialists. Each team member is paid based on their deliverables and shares in the company's profits at the end of the year. As a result, Hoxby is able to operate across time zones and serve clients worldwide.

Collectives are an example of the fluid but coordinated behaviour of ecosystems. Professionals who want to be part of the Hoxby Collective do need to be accepted into the community through an interview and induction process, akin to joining a club. They can then participate and apply freely to be part of the work of the collective, offering their skills whenever and wherever there is an opportunity (which may come through word of mouth or be shared through Hoxby's social media channels), and if they have availability.

Hoxby's culture is built on flexibility, transparency and inclusivity. The WorkStyle approach allows employees to set their own hours and work environment, supporting a fulfilling work–life balance and promoting productivity. Accountability is key in Hoxby's meritocratic system, where workers are judged by the quality of their work, not by the time spent on tasks.

For ecosystemic organizations to work effectively, they require both a new way of organizing (small team or MEs) and a new way of working (captured in the WorkStyle ethos of Hoxby). Alex highlighted to me that Hoxby has learned three important lessons about this new way of working:

1. **Work needs to be done asynchronously, not synchronously** – This means people can add to the work of others without needing to be working at the same time. Shared documents, Slack conversations and similar mechanisms allow for this.

2. **There needs to be a digital-first mentality** – This reduces or removes the requirement for office space altogether and allows much greater sharing and transparency.

3. **A trust-based culture underpins WorkStyle** – In an ecosystem, success is based on outcomes rather than physically presence, so it requires trust that others will deliver and openness of communication to ensure expectations are clear.

To date, Hoxby has used WorkStyle to increase productivity, wellbeing and inclusion. The collective is now promoting WorkStyle's value across businesses and organizations, having clearly seen the positive impact for the company and its customers.

HOW DO WE DELIVER THIS IN PRACTICE?

Many of these examples may seem daunting because we are seeing their success in retrospect. And indeed, in practice, it can be complex to adopt an ecosystem approach in a single "big bang" change effort. However, incremental approaches to change have been effective and fruitful. A colleague has been working with ASA Group, a company that manufactures metal packaging and that has a 65-year history of operating across four countries, with seven production sites. ASA specializes in tinplate steel cans for the chemical, food and aerosol spray sectors. The company currently generates €135 million in turnover. San Marino, Italy, Switzerland and England host ASA's production sites, and the company employs 500 people and collaborates with various external partners. Two of the main directors, Francesco and Michele Amati, have been instrumental to the change. They are pragmatic people working in an industrial environment so they can't afford to be too conceptual in their approach – the ideas need to work.[77]

The group, which began as a family business, has grown through acquisitions over the years. ASA has engaged its internal stakeholders to chart a new course for future growth, aiming to double its turnover between 2024 and 2029. To achieve this, the group's strategy focuses on three key pillars: organic growth in current markets, mergers and acquisitions for expansion, and diversification towards sustainability, with a focus on greener packaging and reduced emissions.

In 2020, ASA faced significant challenges due to the COVID-19 pandemic, leading to the creation of a crisis unit to address operational and logistical issues. This unit eventually evolved into a transformation and re-foundation unit, tasked with re-evaluating how the company operates. ASA realized that its traditional governance mechanisms were insufficient to handle the new reality and embraced an adaptive, ecosystemic approach.

ASA adopted Haier's RenDanHeyi model,[78] which focuses on distributing autonomy, fostering agility and unlocking human potential. The RenDanHeyi model aligns with ASA's desire to shift from a hierarchical, family-run company to a business driven by professional managers with entrepreneurial attitudes. The model also supports empowerment of employees, partners and suppliers, allowing them to contribute to innovation and decision-making.

The RenDanHeyi philosophy has been implemented through several pilot projects at ASA. These include the creation of MEs and EMCs to foster entrepreneurship within the company. For instance, ASA's logistics department transitioned into an ME, offering internal and external logistics services. Another pilot involved digital printing, which shifted from traditional offset-based printing to innovative digital solutions, allowing for more personalized and flexible services. The Oil Millers EMC developed a commercial proposal to address the needs of olive oil millers, aligning multiple internal units to offer customized solutions.

These pilot projects serve as archetypes for how ASA intends to transform its operations. The group supports these initiatives through value adjustment mechanisms, which enable MEs to operate independently while maintaining alignment with the company's strategic goals. The RenDanHeyi model also emphasizes transparency, with financial and performance data shared openly to support decision-making.

As part of its transformation, ASA has moved away from traditional hierarchical management, instead encouraging self-management and peer coordination. Employees now have more autonomy to solve problems and innovate, with profit-sharing mechanisms in place to reward their contributions. The company's new organizational model is designed to be agile, responsive to market changes and capable of driving long-term growth.

ASA's journey towards implementing RenDanHeyi has not been without challenges. Some employees initially found the new model disorienting, but extensive training and experimentation helped them understand its potential. As ASA continues to evolve, it aims to apply the RenDanHeyi principles across the entire organization, including its manufacturing system, to foster a more entrepreneurial, ecosystem-based approach to business.

KEY LEARNING POINTS

- Command-and-control organizations are not fit for purpose for the modern world.

- Network organizations based on ecosystems are essential to future success.

- Nature points us to the key characteristics that make ecosystems sustainable, based on a dynamic equilibrium between growth and maintenance.

- An increasing number of organizations, such as FAVI, are using empowered team-based structures, with strong enabling external and internal relationships as the basis for sustaining growth and innovation.

- A collaborative mindset and enabling structures need to be in place for an ecosystem to be healthy, including leaders who see themselves as 'gardeners' rather than 'directors' and can cultivate the right behaviours and relationships.

APPLICATION EXERCISE

Think about where your organization is now (or you may wish to choose another organization that you have worked with).

Firstly, consider: **what type of structure does your organization currently have** on a scale from bureaucratic command (1) to network (10)?

Secondly, think about **how to enable more of a network structure for your organization** based on the characteristics identified in this chapter:

- **Team-based empowerment:**
    - What would be a logical team structure to base your organization around? An example is a customer-focused team, but note that you will likely need a mix of team types.
    - Are these 'whole work teams' (see *Chapter 6*) that have: a clear purpose; a plan, do and improve cycle; and outcome-based measures?

- **Enablement** – do the teams have the following areas identified in this chapter?
    - Entrepreneurial mindset?
    - Empowering leadership?
    - Shared purpose?

- **Ability to adapt** – does the team have the ability to adapt in the following ways?
    - Respond to changing customer needs (while being close enough to the customer to do this)?
    - Control budgets and the team's own profitability as appropriate to the work?
    - Reward, motivate and attract appropriate staff and skills?

- **Customer-driven incentives:**
  › Are there organization-wide and team-based reward mechanisms that are aligned around sustainable, long-term customer satisfaction?
  › Are the KPIs (key performance indicators) at team level in line with broader organizational aims?

CHAPTER 11

RELEASING CHANGE IN LIVING ORGANIZATIONS

THE OUTSIDER

Barack Obama's origins were inauspicious. He was born on 4 August 1961 in Honolulu, Hawaii, to a Kenyan father, Barack Obama Sr., and an American mother, Ann Dunham. His early childhood was marked by a degree of turbulence. His parents separated when he was two and his father returned to Kenya. Obama lived in Indonesia for several years with his mother and stepfather before returning to Hawaii to live with his maternal grandparents. He attended the Punahou School in Honolulu. As he grew up, he navigated questions of identity and race, fuelled by his own diverse background. These experiences shaped his perspective on multiculturalism and social justice.

He went to Harvard Law School in 1991, where he became the first Black president of the prestigious *Harvard Law Review*. It wasn't until he was 35 that his political career began. In 1996 he was elected to the Illinois Senate, where he served for eight years. During this time, he worked on bipartisan efforts to expand healthcare, reform criminal justice and improve education. His major achievements included legislation on ethics reform and expanding healthcare coverage for children and families.

Despite his intelligence and previous achievements, Obama was not a well-known figure at national level in the USA. A personal turning point came in 2004, when he gained national prominence after delivering a widely praised keynote address at the Democratic National Convention. Later that year, he was elected to the US Senate, representing Illinois. In the Senate, he worked on issues such as government transparency, nuclear non-proliferation and veterans' healthcare, ascending within the Democratic Party. He was still a newcomer and an outsider. In 2006, his initial support in Democratic polls was around 10–20%, with Hillary Clinton polling around 40–50%. However, by 2007 his support had grown to around 25–30%, and by mid-2008 Obama reached about 45–50% in the Democratic primary polls. After he secured the nomination for the presidency in June, his support among Democrats solidified to 60–70%.

In the presidential election, Obama consistently polled around 50%, winning with 52.9% of the vote. So how was he catapulted from being a relatively unknown figure at the start of 2004 to becoming president of the USA at the start of 2009, after winning the 2008 presidential election? He was then re-elected in 2012. The answer lies in his grasp of the nature of change. He created a moment that was driven by strong grassroots campaigning, had a message of change and built on key victories. He recognized that change is about a movement rather than top-down authority.

Figure 26 charts the growth of the movement that propelled Obama to power in the 2008 presidential campaign.[79] It focuses on two years (2007 and 2008) that can be broken down into a number of stages (each roughly of six months):

1. **Full-time team (early 2007):**
    > Assembled a small, experienced team of strategists.
    > Developed the campaign's message: "Hope and Change."
    > Established a data-driven strategy and digital infrastructure.

2. **Local teams (mid-2007 to early 2008):**
    > Set up field offices in key states with full-time organizers.
    > Trained local leaders to manage neighbourhood teams.
    > Decentralized campaign operations to empower community-level organizing.

3. **Volunteers and grassroots movement (2008 primary season):**
   › Mobilized a vast network of volunteers through the MyBO platform and social media.
   › Enabled volunteers to take ownership of organizing, canvassing and spreading the message.
   › Built momentum through grassroots efforts and broad citizen engagement.

4. **Momentum and victory (mid to late 2008):**
   › Transitioned the campaign into a broad social movement.
   › Continued grassroots organizing and voter turnout efforts.
   › Achieved a historic victory in November 2008 by successfully building a nationwide coalition for change.

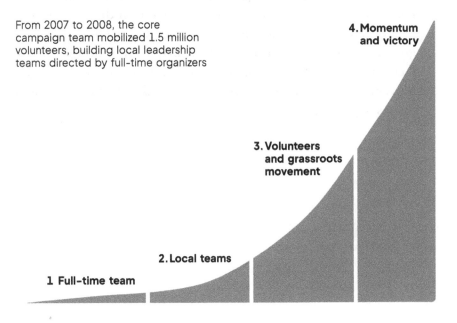

FIGURE 26
Growth of the Obama presidential movement

We can draw lessons and insights from the success of Obama's campaign that are helpful in understanding how successful change happens in society, organizations and markets. These observations include:

- **The forces of change in our world are both more powerful and more diverse than ever**, resulting in a context and circumstances that change quickly.
- **Groups and organizations need to be able to adapt rapidly and continuously** to be successful and deliver messages, products and outcomes that are appropriate to the times.
- **Traditional approaches to change based on top-down command and control are flawed** because they are too slow to adapt and respond to the forces of change.
- However, **movements can grow quickly** because they can quickly reproduce success (e.g. a full team in phase one of the Obama campaign led to tens or hundreds of local teams in the second phase of growth) and unsuccessful approaches can quickly be dropped as the focus is placed on the messages and approaches that are working.
- **Movements grow into networks of relationships** between teams in phases of growth.

CHANGE MOVEMENTS VERSUS TRADITIONAL CHANGE MANAGEMENT

Traditional top-down change approaches have a poor and unenviable record of failure, as illustrated by the following statistics:

- Around 70% of change initiatives fail to achieve their intended outcomes.[80]
- Around 39% of employees resist change due to a lack of understanding and communication about the change.[81]
- Change initiatives that actively engage employees are 30% more likely to succeed.[82]

The view that organizations can be transformed in a top-down fashion is flawed because our view of organizations is flawed. The premise of this book is that organizations are living and made up of a diverse but related group of humans. People form networks of relationships. Successful transformation happens as groups of people think, behave and relate in new ways. This is how transformation movements start, grow and are sustained. So, we need to understand how transformative change movements are triggered and sustained. Change networks and movements have demonstrably more success.

In health, the UK's campaign to reduce drink-driving developed momentum over a series of phases. Beginning in the 1960s, early efforts focused on setting strict legal limits on blood alcohol content. Over time, public awareness grew through initiatives like the Think! campaign, which highlighted the dangers of drink-driving and its consequences. Enforcement measures such as roadside breath tests and harsher penalties strengthened the movement. As awareness spread and enforcement became more rigorous, the impact became evident, with drink-driving deaths decreasing from over 1,600 in the 1970s to around 230 by 2020s, reflecting an 85% reduction. This ongoing movement successfully transformed attitudes and behaviours, dramatically improving road safety.[83]

In business the kaizen movement[84] (introduced in *Chapter 6*), rooted in continuous improvement, originated in Japan after the Second World War, gaining momentum through the Toyota Production System. Toyota applied kaizen to enhance efficiency, emphasizing waste reduction, standardization and employee empowerment. This bottom-up approach encouraged all workers to suggest incremental changes, fostering a culture of improvement. Kaizen expanded beyond Toyota in the 1960s and 1970s, as Japanese businesses adopted it to remain competitive globally. By the 1980s, its success had attracted international attention, especially in the West, where companies integrated kaizen into their own operations. Over time, kaizen evolved from a manufacturing-centric method to a broader business philosophy, impacting diverse sectors such as healthcare, finance and IT. Kaizen's growth has had three phases – initial development at Toyota, nationwide adoption in Japan and global expansion – and it has become a cornerstone of modern lean management practices worldwide.

In society and religion, the story of the growth of the early church as a movement started by Jesus and his disciples is a good example. Jesus began by gathering a core group of disciples, starting with three, expanding to 12 and eventually reaching 72, including both men and women. He articulated the gospel, teaching a new way of living centred on love and service. However, a moment of crisis struck when Jesus was executed, leaving the core group of 12 disciples behind, uncertain of the future.

The movement was reignited when the disciples miraculously encountered Jesus after his resurrection. They now fully understood and embraced the gospel's powerful message. Realizing this was an opportune moment, they began preaching during the festival of Pentecost, sharing the message of Jesus with people from various regions. As these early messengers travelled, they gathered new believers and formed communities. These communities shared a common lifestyle, teachings and testimonies of transformation, including stories of healing and changed lives. They also established new leadership structures that adapted to local cultures.

As the movement grew, new triggers, such as persecution in Jerusalem and meetings with diverse peoples, sparked further expansion. Pioneers like Apostle Paul deliberately took Jesus' message to far-reaching places such as Cyprus, Ephesus and Rome. As they travelled, more communities were established, leading to the formation of what we now recognize as the global Christian church.

CHANGE CHAIN REACTION[85]
CREATING A CHANGE MOVEMENT

What can we learn from these movements to bring about change in our own organizations? The examples illustrate the power and nature of a change network that builds momentum from a small core over time. This is akin to the chain reaction that we see in the world of nuclear energy. In a nuclear fission chain reaction, a neutron hits a heavy atom (such as uranium), causing it to split into two smaller atoms. This releases energy and more neutrons. These neutrons then collide with other heavy atoms, causing further splits. The process repeats, releasing more energy with each split and creating a chain reaction.

I have summarized the growth of a movement in a model of change that I call the Chain Reaction Model. It is illustrated in *Figure 27*.

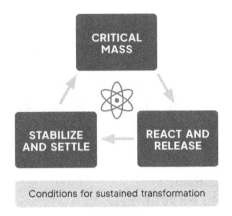

FIGURE 27
Chain Reaction Change model (© Living Work Consulting Ltd 2024)

The elements of the model are:

- **Critical mass** – development of a core team (and later core teams) with a strong shared purpose, behaviours and message.
- **React and release** – the core team engages with wider teams across multiple locations and units.
- **Stabilize and settle** – new teams are established and learn more about the core message and change; they form a wider network of teams connected to their core team.

The chain reaction cycles and iterates, with new teams sharing and living the change, forming a wide network of 'teams of teams' until the whole organization or group is transformed. In the following paragraphs are some of the ways in which these elements play out in practice.

CRITICAL MASS: A CORE CHANGE COMMUNITY

In the various movements, a diverse core team was formed. For instance, the kaizen core team involved managers, engineers, technicians and front-line manufacturing workers who brought different areas of expertise. Obama's core team was made up of David Plouffe (campaign manager), David Axelrod (chief strategist), Robert Gibbs (communications director), Jon Favreau (chief speechwriter), Penny Pritzker (finance chair) and Marshall Ganz (field organizer). This team forged deep relationships and understanding over an intense period of engagement.

Similarly, Jesus spent around three years with his group of 12 disciples, sharing his message in stories and getting them to apply and experiment with his message with various people in various settings. There was intentionality around deep, experience-based learning so the learning would be sustained and embedded with the core group, and they could teach and share with others later in the movement's growth.

REACT AND RELEASE: SPREADING THE MOVEMENT

To reach a point where a movement is ready to spread further, leader(s) need to work out when they have sufficient alignment and understanding in the team to push further. The team needs to be aligned around a core message. Obama's presidential campaign was centred on the themes of "hope" and "change" and had five priorities: unity and bipartisanship, change in Washington, economic reform, healthcare reform and opposition to the Iraq War. This was sufficient to provide a rallying call to his potential supporters and enough substance to give a broad shape to the change. This was then galvanized through speeches, TV appearances, regional meetings and media presence.

Before this stage, the movement had been centred on a small team of leaders and core followers. At this point, regional teams and offices were set up and the message of change could spread in parallel across multiple regions. In this way the movement was primed to form a wider change network. This consists of a group of change agents who are given the essence of the message. In businesses, I have typically done this by training up 'change champions,' who are people who immediately 'get the message' and are keen to play an active role in the movement. When we were propagating a new safety approach and message across a 7,000-strong defence organization, we found certain teams were keen to be the early adopters of the approach. They used the tools and approach we had provided to prove the concept with their projects. They were then change champions, coaches and cheerleaders who helped others in their respective areas of the business (air, sea or land divisions) to begin adopting the approach.

STABILIZE AND SETTLE: SPREADING THE MOVEMENT FURTHER

The 'change reaction' has now started to happen. The react and release stage typically leads to a number of different groups, projects or regions becoming champions of the change. However, like with any reaction, if we don't provide further substance and fuel then the change can burn out. This typically happens when a change is entirely pushed by a central change office rather than allowing new localized change teams to take hold of the change themselves. In addition, it is important that the learnings from the initial stage of the change are captured and formalized to a degree – often in the form of standardized presentations, tools to support the new way of working and processes for building the change into established processes and teams.

In the defence organization, we managed to achieve this in a number of ways, including by:

- Providing a standard video and slide presentation titled "What Is the New Safety Approach?"
- Asking our change champions (early adopter project leads) to give these presentations in their own areas of the business.
- Building the new approach into the selection process for safety engineers and other staff.
- Building key elements into the company management system.
- Dramatizing previous safety incidents, which allowed large numbers of people to see where things had gone wrong in the past, learn from this and understand how the new approach integrated into their roles (as described in *Chapter 4*).

Following on from this initial cycle of critical mass, react and release, and stabilize and settle, the whole cycle can repeat. This time it will happen in multiple places in an organization or ecosystem, ultimately spreading across the whole system.

ENABLERS OF SUCCESSFUL CHANGE MOVEMENTS

Several conclusions can be drawn from these movements about the conditions and enablers that spark the change chain reaction and ensure it continues. Without these, the movement may come to a halt and fail to fulfil its potential. The key enablers include:

- **Plant new teams at each stage** – The key building block of a movement is empowered, local teams. In the Obama campaign, these were based around field offices. In the spread of the Christian church, new communities were formed in each town.
- **Have a compelling message and ensure appropriate timing** – The core message needs to resonate with the audience, be reflected in the behaviour of the core team and have demonstrable impact. The kaizen movement could point to a core set of techniques and significant improvements in productivity. The message also needs to be contextual and timely. In Japan, the scarcity of raw materials following the Second World War meant that the efficiencies and working processes of kaizen were highly attractive.
- **Celebrate stories and small victories** – Never forget the power of a story or testimonial. As part of the UK drink-driving campaign, real stories from those who had lost a family member to a drunk driver were a powerful force for change.
- **Leverage technology and relevant media** – In our modern age, social media can provide a powerful platform to influence opinions among a wider audience. Social media posts can easily go viral as

part of a campaign and act as an accelerant of change. The Obama campaign was a heavy user of social media to share its message of hope and change to galvanize a younger demographic. However, stories and clips can be shared in many forms, from face-to-face testimonials to mass media interviews.

WHAT DOES IT TAKE TO GET THIS WORKING IN PRACTICE?
(A PERSONAL EXAMPLE)

While I was working for a global management consultancy (5,000 consultants), my team and I developed and launched a new global strategic workforce planning (SWP) service. We began as a core team of four and went through three iterations over four years, delivering more than 100 projects. *Figure 28* on the following pages provides an overview of the three iterations and how they followed the chain reaction model.

Initially, I hosted a sharing session with my colleagues to tell the story of a SWP project that I had done for a government client. In this sharing forum, three other colleagues related similar stories of SWP projects – one for a pharmaceutical firm, one for an engineering firm and one for a professional services firm. As a group of four, we extracted insights and experience that we could bring to other clients and summarized these in a client brochure demonstrating the types of SWP services we could offer to help them in their own organizations. Other more junior colleagues at the session helped us and became team members on an early set of three new client projects we won.

Word started to get around our consultancy about this interesting new line of work. One of our recently won projects had enabled our national railway company to deliver the first stage of its Digital Railways strategy. This enabled us to host internal and external events where the client would explain the value of the service to our senior 'seller' colleagues and prospective clients. Alongside this, we formalized a lot of our learning and trained a wider set of consultants. Our core team of four came from different regions (UK, mainland Europe,

Asia and the USA) and we started regional groups to support the new projects we won (while maintaining our core global team).

By the time we had completed a further ten or more projects across different regions, we were ready to go global. We talked to our executive team and presented case studies of 'hero projects' that showed the value of this new service. This enabled us to have global, regional and local marketing efforts going on in parallel. The new service was formally recognized as separate and accounted for on the company systems as a distinct line of business. SWP consulting practice groups met in the regions to share the latest thinking, discuss new project wins and learn. The service had gone from a fledgling group of four consultants to a global practice of over 100 projects with consultants all around the globe able to deliver the projects. The chain reaction had been sustained until the new service had spread throughout the global management consulting firm.

ALIVE

	Iteration 1: initial strategic workforce planning (SWP) consulting projects	Iteration 2: build regional SWP consulting teams	Iteration 3: build a global network of SWP consulting teams
Critical mass	• Formed an initial group of four experienced SWP consultants • Shared past project experience and tools • Created core SWP sales deck and brochure	• Ran SWP training for regional teams • Ran sales enablement for senior sellers to market to clients • Created regional SWP resource teams	• Delivered training to all new consultants on SWP so they could work on projects • Enabled sector and account leads to sell (with tailored materials) • Created global SWP resource team, including regional SWP leads
React and release	• Won three projects with clients • Brought more junior consultants on to learn on projects • Developed new tools on projects	• Launched regional marketing efforts • Resourced new teams, including training consultants • Extended and tailored tools on projects	• Launched global marketing • Launched account and sector-based marketing • Ensured global SWP resource team provided advice, SME resource and tools to projects
Stabilize and settle	• Formalized approach, tools and core training • Identified regional SWP sellers and team members for regional rollout	• Shared regional 'hero project' stories across regional teams • Identified global service leader and supporting teams	• Held regular global and regional SWP team meetings • Consolidated tools, training and case studies • Ongoing learning and knowledge sharing

FIGURE 28
Creating a chain reaction to launch a global service in a management consultancy

KEY LEARNING POINTS

- Traditional change approaches have been shown to be successful no more than 30% of the time, whereas change approaches based on networks and movements are much more likely to succeed.

- Successful change movements vary greatly in size, scale and type; examples include the 2008 Obama-Biden US presidential election campaign, the growth of the kaizen movement and the growth of the early Christian church.

- The Chain Reaction change model provides a framework for considering the stages and ingredients of a successful change movement; it has three process stages:
  - **Critical mass** – building a core change community.
  - **React and release** – ensuring a 'platform for a reaction.'
  - **Stabilize and settle** – supporting new change communities before iterating on a larger scale by building on the earlier stages.

- Underpinning this approach, there is a need to ensure the key conditions and enablers are in place for a change movement to be sustained; they are:
  - Plant new teams at each stage.
  - Ensure there is a compelling message and appropriate timing.
  - Celebrate stories and small victories.
  - Leverage technology and relevant media.

APPLICATION EXERCISE

Thinking of a particular organization, take the Chain Reaction Change Model and work out an action plan for applying it, starting with a small core group.

Work through the following steps, considering the suggested questions below. While doing this, remember to think about the four enablers of change listed at the end of the key learning points.

Critical mass: building a core change community
- What is the core message and aim of the change you are seeking?
- Can you synthesize it to one or two key themes and four to six major aims?
- Who are the initial group? Who represents, owns and lives the change?
- Do you have a good mix of skills in the group (such as a communicator, a logistics lead, a marketer and a financial lead)?
- What can you do to get the core group to represent and experience the change for themselves (e.g. an initial project, offsite learning or visiting others who have done similar work)?
- How will you know that the core team is ready to engage wider stakeholders?
- Where might your initial financial and sponsorship support come from?

React and release: ensuring a 'platform for a reaction'
- How can you encapsulate your core messages and examples in an impactful way (e.g. videos, personal stories or social media posts)?
- Which groups should you approach in the next stage that will become your future core teams (e.g. project teams in each of your organization's main divisions or enthusiasts across different areas)?

- How can you rapidly demonstrate and evidence the impact of the change (e.g. customer testimonies or performance statistics)?
- How can you engage new groups, so they own the change (e.g. coaching support or delivering a project using your approach)?
- What tools and resources will you share with those who get involved?

Stabilize and settle: support the new change communities
- What structures and/or communities will you establish to propagate the change in each of the areas (e.g. hero project teams)?
- What tools and materials do they need to spread the change (e.g. video messages, case studies of their own work or tools to deliver/tailor the approach locally)?
- What support and mentoring from original change leaders will enable the new change communities to learn these lessons quickly?
- How will you ensure that each new group is healthy and growing sufficiently so that it will eventually trigger a new reaction?

Finally, review *Figure 28* and complete a similar grid for your organization, giving a clear title to each iteration and consider key activities at each stage of the change chain reaction (critical mass, react and release, and stabilize and settle) based on the example in this chapter.

SECTION C

SHAPING AND
BUILDING LIVING
ORGANIZATIONS

CHAPTER 12

ILLNESS AND HEALTH IN LIVING ORGANIZATIONS

ANOTHER BRICK IN THE WALL

From the age of five, I was entranced by Lego. It started with the big blocks – Duplo – but graduated to the classic smaller Lego blocks. I was building everything from oil rigs to small towns. When Lego Technic appeared, I graduated to vehicles with working engines, suspensions and steering columns. This was the 1980s into the early 1900s. Yet this beloved brick-building empire almost crumbled (bad pun, sorry!) in the early 2000s. Lego was in deep financial trouble, trying to be too many things at once. Having built great toy block sets, the company had got thinking, "Hey, let's run a theme park and throw some Lego-branded t-shirts into the mix?" It was a mess.

THE GREAT LEGO COMEBACK
By the late 1990s, Lego had stretched itself too thin. Between theme parks, video games and apparel (because who wouldn't want a Lego shirt, right?), it lost focus on what made it special: the bricks. Meanwhile, kids were ditching toys for video games and Lego was struggling to keep up. In 2003, they lost almost $220 million. The road to bankruptcy was ahead.

HOW DID LEGO SNAP BACK INTO SHAPE?
The story took a turn when Jørgen Vig Knudstorp became Lego's new CEO in 2004. Knudstorp decided to stop chasing every new opportunity and focused on the purpose of Lego – making awesome building blocks that spark creativity and imagination. Instead of trying to be the Swiss army knife of toy companies, they homed in on what made them great.

They dusted off the classics and introduced new products that stayed true to the company's heart. This was summed up in their purpose statement: "To inspire and develop the builders of tomorrow."[86]

To achieve this, Knudstorp worked to build cohesive alignment in leadership teams and culture by decentralizing decision-making and empowering leaders to act quickly and strategically. He encouraged the development of products such as Lego Architecture, created by cross-functional teams based on customer feedback. Lego Architecture allowed budding builders to recreate anything from Notre Dame in Paris to the Taj Mahal in India. Knudstorp instilled a growth mindset, promoting experimentation and innovation while aligning leaders with Lego's core values of creativity and imagination. He also invested in leadership development and succession planning to ensure future leaders would carry on this approach.

Another key step was to create a flexible and responsive organization. Bureaucracy had stifled Lego's creativity, so teams were given more autonomy and room to experiment. This led to breakthrough products such as Lego Mindstorms (reconfigurable, self-build robots, anyone?). Small, flexible teams with their own budgets were able to quickly adapt to changing customer demands, tailoring products to what different regions wanted.

Finally, Knudstorp refocused the company on Lego's core capabilities. A major lesson learned was to stick to what you're good at. Lego sold off its theme parks and divested everything that didn't align with its 'brick-building' mission. This sharpened focus on innovation led to blockbuster products such as Lego Star Wars, and Lego Harry Potter – because what's better than combining the power of the Force or a magic wand with building blocks?

THE HAPPY ENDING

By 2008, Lego was not only back in business but also thriving. It has experienced tremendous growth, with its revenue increasing from around $1 billion to over $7 billion by 2022, making it the world's largest toy manufacturer. The company expanded its market reach globally, significantly grew its customer base through popular product lines such as Lego Star Wars and more than tripled its workforce to support increased innovation and demand.

So, what's the moral of the story? Like a well-balanced person, don't try to be everything to everyone. Sometimes, all you need is a few blocks and a good imagination to build something amazing again!

ILLNESS IN ORGANIZATIONS

As humans, we inherently understand the need for health in all the dimensions of our being and the interconnected nature of health. The mental health epidemic during the COVID-19 pandemic brought home the multidimensional nature of human health. Many people took to physical exercise to address their mental as well as physical health needs. With young people, parents and teachers focus on helping them to find a sense of purpose, which typically leads to improved emotional mood, a better mindset and greater physical motivation.

In the Lego case study above, we saw how organizations reflect the human need for purpose and its expression in our emotional, cognitive and physical being. The new CEO, Knudstorp, acted as a type of 'organizational doctor,' identifying four important symptoms of ill-health in the company. Building on the information in the case study above, these were:

- **Losing the magic of purpose** – Lego had started doing everything from t-shirts to rollercoasters and had forgotten about those small blocks that children (and adults!) loved to innovate and build with.
- **Losing sight of 'what we are great at'** – Why didn't I play with Meccano all the time as a kid? Lego provided incredible flexibility around a unique, core design of construction parts. They had efficient plants to fabricate a wide array of pieces and a global supply chain that saw them in shops from Baltimore to Brighton.

- **Becoming rigid and unresponsive** – While Lego had lost focus on its purpose, it had also grown to become a bureaucratic structure that ploughed on with ventures that were neither successful commercially nor built on the unique competencies of its employees. It had to sell its theme parks to Merlin Entertainments (who did have the right competencies) after large losses. It also created a clothing and lifestyle brand that included clothes, shoes, lunchboxes, home décor and various bags. The rigidity of the company meant that an expensive and expansive brand was built without quickly recognizing that these products lacked the magic and appeal of the core product.
- **Failing to engage around a single vision** – Lego's leadership around 2000 was characterized as autocratic and top down while also lacking a clear sense of direction. The leadership was acting more like a 'team of managers' (as discussed in *Chapter 4*) than a unified 'enterprise leadership,' with each having an agenda for their function. Lego had implicitly represented a set of core values – creativity, fun, learning, care and quality – that the business had lost sight of. Employees were proud of seeing kids around the world create brand new worlds lost in imagination and play. A Lego t-shirt was never going to represent these core values and vision. So, engagement and morale steadily reduced.

BECOMING AN ORGANIZATIONAL DOCTOR

The areas discussed in the previous section are representative of ill-health in an organization in each of the four dimensions introduced in *Chapters 3 and 4*: purpose, cognitive, physical and emotional. We have the opportunity as consultants, leaders, employees and stakeholders to seek out the symptoms of ill-health in organizations early to avoid future impacts. Just like a doctor spotting that someone's diet is going to lead to diabetes, we can spot symptoms like overdiversification that might lead to poor financial results and loss of employee morale. *Figure 29* introduces a range of typical symptoms and links them to a likely diagnosis and potential 'treatments.'

Chapter 12 — Illness and health in living organizations

	SYMPTOMS (ISSUE)	DIAGNOSIS (NEED)	RESTORING HEALTH (TREATMENT)
PURPOSE	• Disparate lines of business • Overdiversification • Lack of prioritization of where to focus (money, time and energy)	• Get back to the basics – learn from organizational history • Sum up purpose succinctly	• Speak to customers, employees and shareholder about 'who we are' • Develop purpose, mission and core value statements • Prioritize investment in core ventures and divest others
COGNITIVE	• Core skills and competencies not clear or not maintained • Future skills focus not lined up with purpose and aims	• Identify core capabilities and develop them in employees through partnerships and acquisitions	• Identify core capabilities linked to strategy and purpose • Introduce a development and sourcing strategy
PHYSICAL	• Inflexible structures • Inability to react to customers and market quickly	• Introduce empowered team-based structures • Get close to the customer with devolved decision-making	• Empower people and teams with flatter, market-driven structures (e.g. teams, mini-enterprises) • Align team measures to customer outcomes (even internal teams)
EMOTIONAL	• Low employee engagement • Poor morale • Blame and toxic culture	• Engage the workforce in a powerful purpose and empower them to make a difference	• Systematically develop communication and engagement skills in leaders • Give people real power and tools that can make a difference

FIGURE 29
Organizational illness and health: from symptoms to treatments

Most of us don't get the opportunity to completely reshape the organizations we work with or for. However, as we reach greater seniority and gather experience, opportunities will arise that allow us to help make our workplaces sites where people can flourish and deliver their best. As soon as we have spent any significant time in a workplace, we can, with a trained eye, see where there is ill-health in our teams and organization. *Figure 29* gives us some typical symptoms to look for. We can then find opportunities to help our organization and leadership move towards becoming a living organization. In the following sub-sections, I share a few experiences where consulting teams that I've led have managed to achieve just that. I hope this will provide some inspiration for your journey as an 'organizational doctor.'

STORY 1:
BOTTLING PURPOSE AT AN ASSET MANAGEMENT FIRM

Focus: Sustaining purpose, behaviours and value

When I first walked into the office, I heard the gentle buzz of conversation and laughter alongside an industrious group of office workers huddled around desks and open areas. The office looked out over the London skyline with the wonderful architecture of St Paul's Cathedral and the City of London in view. I could detect a warmth and focus to the interactions between people even before I got to know them in my role as a consultant. They had grown steadily over several years doing a mix of retail, commercial and residential real estate projects – mostly but not exclusively in the private sector. They had several billion pounds of assets that they had developed and now managed. They had also spawned a supporting business to help commercial and retail clients with their marketing. Despite the high value of the assets, the total number of staff was under 300.

I met with two directors and the heads of HR and marketing. The conversation was along the lines of "We've got a great bunch of people here and we're proud of what we've achieved. However, we can feel that we're beginning to break off into our own tribes and working increasingly separately. We want to keep the spark that we felt strongly when there were just 20 or so of us." They had the experience and understanding to see the importance of purpose and a shared vision.

WHAT DID WE DO?

I had the good fortune of speaking to the organizational development leader at British Airways when they were trying to tackle similar issues. His advice was simple: "It must come from the heart – a summing up of what people feel about the organization at its best." So, at the asset management firm, we began running focus groups with cross-sections of employees and leaders across the business. We then spoke to a few customers to ask them "What's great about working with this firm?" We made a few videos with people that we used to prompt discussion and reflection (and ultimately for communications). As described in *Chapter 3*, we first synthesized purpose (the why), then the values (what) and then behaviours (how).

The outputs are summarized (at a high level) in *Figure 30*. We found that the staff were proud of the 'urban destinations' they had created where people could live, go to wonderful local restaurants, enjoy some peace in a garden area, go to shops and enjoy experiences (such as cinemas and theatres). As a result, they chose to develop unique brands for these destinations, reflecting the identity that each of them had.

"We create urban destinations and experiences that build sustainable communities"		
1. Power to the People	**2. Design It Better**	**3. Deliver Well**
Trust one another	Simplify things	Take responsibility
Be yourself	Challenge the status quo	Identify solutions
Involve and cooperate	Prioritize the essentials	Achieve outcomes

FIGURE 30
Purpose, values and behaviours of the asset management firm

Leaders and staff alike were most proud of the place of work that they had created. One member of staff, Anne, related a story about her first few weeks and her boss, Ian. Anne had come from a similar firm that pushed hard for short-term financial results. It was an environment in which she felt she couldn't make mistakes. Around three weeks into working at this new firm, Ian had said, "Anne, it's alright if your new property concept doesn't work first time – we'll just iterate it together. You're allowed to try and fail here." She relaxed and delivered! This led to the value "Power to the People" with its emphasis on trusting colleagues and being authentic and cooperative.

WHAT WAS THE RESULT?

Probably the result that I was proudest of was that one of the directors (originally a sceptic) said to us, "You've managed to bottle the magic of this place. Thank you!" The company chose to take the values and embed them in both its external (customer) and internal (employee) communications and processes. During attraction, induction and recruitment, it brought the purpose and values alive in videos, communications and processes. It became clearer about which behaviours it was looking for in new recruits and how these were more important than some specific technical skills.

WHAT DID WE LEARN?

Purpose and life come from the heart. Organizations are typically founded with a strong sense of purpose and core values held by one or more founders. However, as with the Lego example, these can atrophy over time unless we 'bottle the purpose' and repeatedly remind our colleagues of it, sharing with them what we value and how we behave together. This must be embedded in all we do and truly owned. It is a constant process of renewal.

STORY 2:
SHAPING A DIGITAL COMMS AND TECHNOLOGY WORKFORCE AT A GLOBAL OIL AND GAS FIRM

Focus: Developing cognitive skills aligned with the purpose of the function

The firm was vast, employing nearly 90,000 people globally. Even the UK base for the digital comms and technology (DCT) and business staff that we worked at had more than 3,500 people on site. Over 2,000 employees and a further 1,000 or more contractors worked for the global CIO. The purpose of the DCT workforce was (at the top level) clear – "deliver the current and future DCT services that the global organization needs." However, the organization had grown rapidly in recent years, responding to conflicting requests from around the world, and had lost its connection to its core purpose. There were nearly 150 people doing web development despite the firm having a web provider. The alignment with purpose and ultimate aims was missing.

WHAT DID WE DO?

Our first port of call was working with the DCT leadership team. The CIO worked with his senior team to clarify their aims and priorities in light of the wider aims of the organization. They articulated six broad aims and gave substance to the purpose and strategy and how they would be delivered. With clarity around these aims, the DCT organizational 'body' had a direction and a future shape within which to develop. The fundamental capabilities could then be linked into aims so people had clarity about roles, skills and ways of working. We fleshed this out, simply using a strategy-mapping technique to provide a high-level guide for all the DCT staff. The resulting mapping is shown in *Figure 31* on the next page.

The mapping shows how purpose and strategic goals were linked to people capabilities in the organization. For instance, there was a desire to deliver better IT services to users. This included support for mobile devices, laptops, personal computers and access to the company systems. There was a lack of consistency and standardization of these services. So, a standard (ITIL, or Information Technology Infrastructure Library) of consistent service delivery processes was adopted and teams were organized around this. Roles were given consistent titles such as service delivery manager, process development manager and operations analyst, as well as training in how to deliver consistent and high-quality services. Staff could be measured against the competencies for these roles and given personal development plans.

ALIVE

Business strategy

IT Strategy

| Ensure secure connectivity anywhere | Simplify data and applications architecture | Reduce cost and improve delivery speed of applications development | Manage projects consistently and effectively | Standardize service delivery and service support approach | Build clear relationship management with business |

Critical processes

| Security management and risk assessment | Architectural design | Applications development management | Project lifecycle management | ITIL service delivery and support processes | Requirements capture |

Enabling capability

| Digital security | Architecture | Applications | Project management | Service delivery | Information strategy |

Capacity – roles

| • Digital security manager
• Digital risk manager | • Enterprise architect
• Domain architect | • Development manager
• Applications manager | • Programme director
• Project manager | • Operations analyst
• Process development manager | • Information manager
• Process expert |

Competence – skills

| • Digital risk assessment
• Digital standards and regulation | • Architectural analytics
• Marketing technology | • Applications lifecycle management
• Applications portfolio management | • Project benefits management
• Project planning and control | • Configuration management
• Capacity management
• User support | • Leading and managing change
• Business synchronization |

● Good capability ● Fair capability ○ Poor capability

FIGURE 31
Mapping the strategy to the future capabilities in the DCT organization

What emerged from this mapping was a picture of the parts of the DCT 'body' and what they needed to be capable of. Evolution and development could then happen within these areas to achieve the overall mission, giving direction to people's efforts. For instance, the close relationship needed between the business customer and the DCT organization (to capture requirements) required an information strategy capability. In conversations and workshops, it was clear that this involved two specific areas of expertise: process experts, who could map the business to technology requirements, and information strategy partners, who could then build the result into a requirement for the DCT organization to deliver. These groups were then broken out into career paths with supporting development (theory and practice) to grow their competencies and ways of working.

WHAT WAS THE RESULT?

The immediate satisfaction was to see new technology communities of practice grow. The IT project management community aligned themselves around a way of delivering projects consistently, gaining project qualifications as they progressed and establishing an identity through regular conference-style meetings where project learnings and successes were shared. An emerging expertise in IT security, which has since become essential, led to new innovations and the establishment of an industry IT security standard. Career paths and a development portal brought the learning journey alive, benefitting employees through their personal growth and the organization through expertise in the areas needed to realize company ambitions. The work was featured in a leading computing journal.

WHAT DID WE LEARN?

Living organizations need local freedom with a core framework (we might think of this as their skeleton). Once purpose and aims are clear, we need to provide a framework for growth and the freedom to use the purpose and aims individually and within teams.

STORY 3:
SHAPING STRUCTURES AROUND THE CUSTOMER IN A HEALTHCARE SYSTEM

Focus: Aligning physical processes and structure to the needs of patients (purpose)

Health becomes an increasing priority for most of us as we age. Many older people develop ongoing issues in areas such as heart disease, diabetes and arthritis. Alongside this, many experience dementia and cognitive decline, which affect memory and decision-making abilities. Lack of mobility can lead to a level of social isolation that affects mental and physical health. On the positive side, there are legions of healthcare professionals, social care professionals and volunteers who seek to make this stage of life enjoyable and ensure people are well supported. However, the sheer number and variety of organizations – including the likes of Help the Aged, the UK's National Health Service (NHS) acute hospitals, GPs and community healthcare providers – can mean people and needs get missed as each organization 'does its own thing.' How can we ensure the patient remains at the centre of solutions?

When I was working as a director of the organizational consultancy Tricordant, we were confronted by exactly this issue when we were engaged by a UK county council working with various NHS bodies and charities around how best to treat and support elderly people.[87] They were struggling with various difficulties, including the following:

- When an elderly person had even a minor physical issue outside normal working hours (when GPs were unavailable), they tended to go to hospital, clogging up capacity for others more in need.
- Health and social care acted independently. An elderly person would come out of hospital after a fall in the home, but no assessment would be available of the suitability of their environment and care (something that social care would typically do). This was necessary to ensure they didn't fall again and therefore end up in hospital again soon after.
- Local charities had wonderful volunteers and resources that were often not being directed to the needs that health and social care workers didn't have the time or resources to cover. These volunteers could perform an essential role in integrating an elderly person into the local community by providing transport and communications and putting on relevant events. This would help support their physical, mental and emotional health.

WHAT DID WE DO?

Living organisms of all types respond to their environment, adapting and shaping themselves to that environment. A classic example is the chameleon, which changes to match the colour of its environment to disguise itself and protect itself from predators. Living organizations do the same with their customers – starting with an external (customer) perspective. Working with the core stakeholders (across NHS bodies, County Council and 3rd Sector Groups), we began with the stages of the patient journey shown in *Figure 32* on the next page.

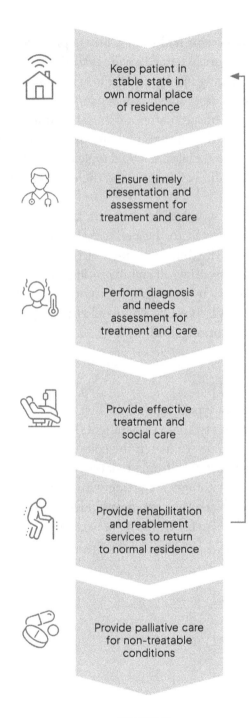

FIGURE 32
Stages of the patient journey

A patient moves along a pathway. Initially, they are in stable health in their normal place of residence. When they show signs of illness, it is important that they connect with the health system through speaking to their GP, accessing healthcare through the internet or contacting another relevant healthcare facility. Diagnosis should follow in a timely manner, with tests being run to understand the cause of the illness before the patient moves on to appropriate treatment (potentially in hospital). An important step is then their discharge back to their normal place of residence. A particular focus is what health and social care practitioners call "reablement and rehabilitation," which means ensuring that they will be safe and stable on their return. This might involve regular social care visits or adjustments to a home environment. For some elderly people, it is clear that their condition is not treatable so they should be moved on to palliative care (relief from pain and other symptoms) in an environment that best serves them and their family (maybe their home or a hospice).

It was important to look at this process through the eyes of the patient and consider the specific outcomes (we called them "significant events") that needed to happen at each stage of the journey. There was an opportunity to address the delays and issues that patients experienced during this process, causing them anxiety and making the system incur additional cost as people were dealt with ineffectively. In this health and social care system – which could involve up to 150 leaders and staff from various organizations, collaborating to find better solutions – we brought together the 'whole system' to walk through the patient journey and look at how to improve.

WHAT WAS THE RESULT?

The multi-organization group came up with improvement ideas such as a non-emergency response service (like the 111 number in the UK, versus 999 for acute emergencies). New teams and structures were created, including multidisciplinary teams. Combined social and healthcare worker teams collaborated on the patient's return to their home (so a proper assessment could be done by both groups). This required new ways of working across organizational boundaries, as an ecosystem. It became a holistic solution affecting the physical processes and structures as well as requiring new skills and knowledge and ways of working together.

WHAT DID WE LEARN?

Living systems are able to work together as a whole. One part of a body (such as a hand) doesn't say to another (such as an arm), "I don't need you." In the same way, living organizations must be able to respond as a whole to patients' needs. We saw a similar example in *Chapter 1* where we looked at the team-based Buurtzorg health and social care organization, where multidisciplinary teams work with patients in a given geographical area. By organizing and structuring around the six key areas of the patient journey in *Figure 32*, we were able to empower teams to address issues and improve the way that they helped patients.

STORY 4:
ALIGNING A LEADERSHIP TEAM AT A SATELLITE AGENCY

Focus: Engaging leadership and employees to have a shared purpose and ways of working (emotional connection to purpose

It felt like walking into the headquarters of the Thunderbirds. There were screens across the walls with images of satellites and moving dots representing their positions. Operators sat at screens and keyboards with headsets speaking to fellow operators in other countries.

I was at the HQ of a European satellite agency that launched, maintained and exploited a pan-European system of operational satellites. It had grown from a small start-up organization in 1986 to a major agency operating multiple types of satellites on behalf of 30 European nations. In the process, it had moved from a tight team that ate and worked together over long days to a set of separate functions that the previous CEO had tried to manage directly even as it grew larger. However, the industry was shifting from custom design to agile assembly of standard components from industry suppliers. A new long-term (20-year) strategy was required based on new assumptions while returning to the clarity of purpose from the early days.

WHAT DID WE DO?
The starting point was working with the top team around a renewed purpose, building a shared set of priorities for the next 20 years in a rapidly changing space market. This required new behaviours, high levels of trust and total alignment about strategic direction. We undertook

stakeholder interviews and designed and delivered sessions for the whole top team at the company's European HQ. Together they worked, with our facilitation, to develop a team purpose statement, establish top-team meeting and work behaviours, forge a deep understanding of one another (beyond their immediate work) and set out their strategic priorities. The focus was on becoming a single 'controlling mind' for the rapidly growing enterprise, providing clarity and energy to the wider staff.

WHAT WAS THE RESULT?

After the work, the director general said: "Our leadership team has developed a shared sense of purpose, values and ways of working. Our strategic planning is, for the first time, centred around a shared purpose and priorities. It's helping us deliver our strategy with far less friction and much greater cohesion than in the past."

WHAT DID WE LEARN?

You're never too old to learn new tricks. All the people involved were enormously experienced in their functional areas, often sought after across the European space industry but less experienced at different ways of working in larger, more complex organizations. However, they created an environment in which people could listen to one another and rediscover their passion for the 'mission' (often a literal space mission!). They showed great flexibility in shaping new ways of working that would better achieve the mission in the new context.

WHAT'S IN THE DOCTOR'S BAG?

As we work at improving our own organizations, we need to think more like an organizational doctor who helps others to diagnose organizational health. Like any doctor, we need to consider what we put in our medical bag to support our colleagues and help them develop. *Figure 33* on the next page introduces some examples (not exhaustive) of the types of questions and tools that might feature in that kit.

ALIVE

PURPOSE	
Useful Questions	**Useful Tools and Concepts**
Do we have a simple phrase that sums up why we are in business?	Why? What? How? Structure of purpose, values and behaviour
Do we understand our core values and the behaviours we are committed to?	
Do we know our priorities and the big goals we are all committed to?	Audacious goals

COGNITIVE	
Useful Questions	**Useful Tools and Concepts**
Have we got the skills we need for our future?	Future skills strategy map (Figure 31)
How can we embrace technology to help us think smarter and quicker?	AI tools

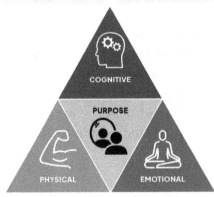

PHYSICAL	
Useful Questions	**Useful Tools and Concepts**
Are the structures and processes linked back to the purpose and core value chain?	Value Chain.
Do we have dynamic and flexible structures that enable continuous growth and improvement?	Whole Work Team Principles and different improvement team structures (agile, kaizen, etc.)

EMOTIONAL	
Useful Questions	**Useful Tools and Concepts**
Do we feel engaged with colleagues and the organization?	Engagement surveys
Can we articulate what is special about the culture and working here?	Culture diagnostics

FIGURE 33
Questions and tools that might form part of an organizational doctor's medical bag

Chapter 12 — Illness and health in living organizations

As part of your own journey applying the ideas and insights from this book, I would recommend you consider what you see as the essential elements of this organizational doctor's medical bag.

KEY LEARNING POINTS

- Organizations, like people, can get 'ill' and stray from what made them successful in the first place, so we need to think like organizational doctors.

- Organizations are whole and we need to look at symptoms like poor employee engagement, customer dissatisfaction, poor profitability and excessive bureaucracy to identify patterns of dysfunction or 'illness.'

- By applying the living organization framework discussed throughout this book, we can understand the underlying issues that are causing the problems and link them to potential solutions.

- Solutions, like doctors' patients, are contextual, and they must be appropriate to the organization, depending on the organization's stage of development and its unique combination of symptoms.

- We can use a core set of diagnostic approaches and measures (as outlined in *Figure 33*) to 'take the temperature' of an organization as a rapid way of identifying the priorities to address.

APPLICATION EXERCISE

Consider an organization that you are working in or with. For this organization, what questions and tools do you want in your organizational doctor's medical bag? Refer to *Figure 33* as a starting point and build up your own set of questions and tools.

CHAPTER 13

YOUR JOURNEY TO A LIVING ORGANIZATION

INTREPID TRAVELS

Our children were in their early teens and becoming increasingly curious about the wider world. Most of their experience was of various parts of England, where we live, with occasional holidays to other European countries for a week or two. Our younger daughter was developing a strong sense of justice and aversion to inequality in the world, aware that children in other countries didn't have the same opportunities.

All of this led us to the decision that it would be wonderful to go on a different kind of travel experience, close to a non-European culture. We chose to go to Vietnam to see the full extent of the country, from Hanoi in the north right down to the Mekong Delta in the south (beyond Ho Chi Minh City, formerly Saigon). In the process, we were immersed in the history and culture of a land with beautiful scenery and seascapes and a vibrant economy that has managed to recover from the ravages of the ferocious Vietnam War. We were able to stay in the jungle and eat a number of meals with a Vietnamese family. We ate local foods, saw famous temples and navigated the Mekong Delta in long tail boats. Our guide was a local Thai person, Bo, whose father had been in the Viet Cong (freedom fighters) against the US forces in the war but who now enjoyed taking American tourists around his country. Rich conversations and experiences ensued.

Chapter 13　　　　　　　　　　　　　　　　　　Your journey to a living organization

All of this was possible because of a company called Intrepid Travel, which was founded by Darrell Wade and Geoff Manchester in 1989.[88] Intrepid Travel is a great illustration of the journey that goes into building a living organization as it illustrates how to develop and maintain a thriving organization as it grows. We will draw out a series of discovery questions – which build on the ideas throughout this book – as we review Intrepid's story.

Wade and Manchester were fuelled by a shared vision, founding the company with the purpose of providing immersive, responsible travel experiences. Rather than traditional tourism that prioritized comfort and conventional sightseeing, Intrepid aimed to deliver real-life adventures that connected travellers with local cultures and supported sustainable tourism. This mission quickly set them apart in an industry focused on all-inclusive, sanitized tours. For Intrepid, responsible tourism – minimizing environmental impact while fostering genuine cultural exchanges – was not a marketing angle but a core value. They had answered the **first living organization discovery question: do we know why we exist?**

The company's unique capabilities emerged early on, particularly their commitment to sustainability and cultural immersion. They organized small-group tours that used local resources, stayed in locally owned and run accommodation, and partnered with guides from the communities people were visiting. The aim was to avoid the 'bubble' effect of conventional tours, encouraging travellers to engage deeply with local ways of life. By setting this foundation, Intrepid fostered strong customer loyalty and positive word of mouth, laying the groundwork for expansion. They were answering the **second living organization discovery question: do we have the capabilities to live our purpose?**

Intrepid's expansion in the mid-1990s was deliberate and values driven. As demand grew, they gradually added destinations across Asia and later extended to Africa and the Americas. Their strategy focused on carefully managing growth while maintaining their mission, which meant resisting the urge to scale up at the cost of sustainability. They continued with small-group tours and forged new partnerships with local suppliers to create economic opportunities for host communities. This approach helped them stand out in a growing field of adventure travel, attracting a dedicated customer base that shared their values. By the late 1990s, they were operating in over 20 countries, and annual revenue was steadily increasing.

As the company matured, so did its organizational structure. Wade and Manchester's leadership style was collaborative and inclusive, embodying a culture of open communication and ethical decision-making. Rather than a top-down approach, they encouraged employees to actively participate in shaping Intrepid's direction, fostering a sense of shared ownership of the company's mission. This culture of inclusion extended to travellers and community partners, creating a strong network of stakeholders invested in Intrepid's success. They were answering the **third living organization discovery question: how do we create adaptive living structures and environments in which people thrive?**

During the 2000s, Intrepid adapted to industry shifts by diversifying their offerings. They introduced new types of trips, including family adventures and specialized culinary tours. By 2010, Intrepid was operating in 90 countries and generating approximately $65 million in revenue annually. The company reached a major milestone that same year by becoming carbon neutral – a move that underscored their commitment to sustainability. This achievement not only positioned them as leaders in responsible travel but also reinforced their brand identity in the eyes of environmentally conscious travellers. They were showing they could answer the **fourth living organization discovery question: can we recognize when we need to embrace the next major stage of development?**

In 2015, Intrepid took a bold step by becoming a certified B Corp, committing to rigorous standards of social and environmental performance. This certification aligned with their mission to balance profit with purpose, marking a new phase in their organizational development. The B Corp status strengthened Intrepid's reputation as an ethical travel provider, helping to attract partnerships with like-minded organizations and deepen their impact. The company also invested heavily in the Intrepid Foundation, their non-profit arm, which has since contributed over $12 million to community projects. By this time, Intrepid was moving into fully embracing a wider ecosystem of partners, answering the **fifth living organization discovery question:**

how do we embrace wider relationships and partnerships to remain dynamic and relevant to the future?

Today (late 2024), Intrepid operates over 1,000 itineraries across 120 countries, drawing more than 350,000 travellers annually. Their revenue reached $500 million in 2023, establishing them as the world's largest adventure travel company. Yet, their commitment to responsible travel remains unchanged. Through a culture of ethical leadership, stakeholder inclusion and unwavering dedication to sustainability, Intrepid continues to redefine what it means to be a travel company that cares for the world and its communities. Intrepid doesn't know exactly what the future holds but they have shown to date how they have answered critical questions that enable them to be 'fully alive'!

LINKING BACK TO OUR LIVING ORGANIZATION PRINCIPLES

We saw in *Chapter 2* that life is underpinned by seven key characteristics that living organizations should reflect if they are to grow and thrive long term. We can practically engage with these in our own organizations by using the discovery questions introduced in the Intrepid case study. They are shown in *Table 10* on the next page, which links the characteristics of living organizations with the broad discovery questions so you can use the questions to initiate discussion and diagnosis in your own situation.

LIVING ORGANIZATION CHARACTERISTIC	DISCOVERY QUESTION
1. **Purpose driven** Driven by unique purpose and identity	Do we know why we exist?
2. **Cognitive/physical/emotional embodiment of core identity** In skills, structure and culture	Do we have the capabilities to live our purpose?
3. **Capability based** Unique skills and culture	
4. **Adaptation** Changing over time	How do we create adaptive living structures and environments in which people thrive?
5. **Integration/balance** Through cross-cutting mechanisms	
6. **Lifelong growth** Growing and developing over life stages	Can we recognize when we need to embrace the next major stage of development?
7. **Network** Linked across different units into wider alliances, networks and platforms	How do we embrace wider relationships and partnerships to remain dynamic and relevant to the future?

TABLE 10
Living organization discovery questions

In the final sections of this chapter, I will share some experiences and hints about how best to engage in this discovery process with your own organization and team, often linking back to the practical application exercises introduced in the related chapters of this book.

DISCOVERY QUESTION 1:
DO WE KNOW WHY WE EXIST?

As Victor Frankl relates in his book *Man's Search for Meaning*, a person's most fundamental quest is for meaning and purpose.[89] The same is true for teams, organizations and whole communities as they answer the question, "Why do we exist?" The work of Jim Collins and Jerry Porras in *Built to Last* teaches us that long-term financial success also depends on this sense of purpose (see *Chapter 3*).[90] Intrepid Travel summed up their purpose in the statement "to create positive change through the joy of travel." This reflects their commitment to offering meaningful travel experiences that foster cultural exchange, support local communities and promote environmental sustainability.

Chapter 3 introduced a simple framework to help you develop your organization's core purpose based on answering the questions 'Why?' (purpose), 'What?' (shared values) and 'How?' (behaviours), as shown back in *Figure 3*.

What are some practical ways of answering these questions within your organization? From my own and others' experience, I would offer the following advice:

1. **Focus on why (core purpose)** – Initiate a conversation with employees and other key stakeholders asking why they work for you and what gets them out of bed in the morning. Purpose is discovered rather than created from scratch. Useful questions to discuss include:
    > Share a story about when you felt really proud to work here – why was this?
    > How do we make people's lives better?
    > What is unique about us that we enable?

2. **Uncover shared beliefs (values)** – People love to work with others who have positive, human values. Existing and emerging organizations will already have good examples of these (as well as some disappointing examples). The focus is again on uncovering the best aspects of your organization (or what you aspire to). Potential questions include:
    > What do you really value about working here?
    > How might you express this as a single word or phrase (with a brief explanation)?

3. **What does this look like in day-to-day experience (behaviours)** – While it's important to share a purpose and values, these need to be part of daily working life. Behaviours are how purpose and values 'show up' and how you become the company you aspire to be. Consider the following questions:
    > Considering each of the organization's values in turn, can you share a recent story where someone expressed the values in their day-to-day working life?
    > What name and definition would you give to this behaviour?
    > How can you make each value more explicit?
    > In what ways can you embed this into your culture more deeply?

DISCOVERY QUESTION 2:
DO WE HAVE THE CAPABILITIES TO LIVE OUR PURPOSE?

Chapter 5 defined a capability as the "combination of people, processes, technology, organization and ways of working that enables a firm to deliver an outcome." As we saw, Amazon "seeks to be Earth's most customer-centric company, where customers can find and discover anything they want to buy online," and it does this through four core capabilities: customer interface design, supply chain management, customer relationship and relevance, and technological innovation.

In our own lives, we find meaning and purpose in doing the things that we are naturally good at – in other words, using our capabilities (strengths, skills, knowledge, mindset and outlook). For instance, I love to help people and organizations make their visions real, and I have strengths in seeing the big picture, communicating ideas and motivating people to action. Similarly, organizations have (through their founders and early recruits) and develop capabilities to realize what they are passionate about. To make this clearer for your own organization and focus your development approach, consider the following questions:

1. What is our purpose and customer value proposition?

2. What is the set of capabilities (perhaps four or five) that will enable us to deliver our strategy?

3. For each capability:
   a. What is it?
   b. Why is it valuable?
   c. How is it different from today?
   d. What does it look like in action?
   e. What is required to make it happen?

4. For all of the capabilities:
   a. What investment do we need to make, and can we justify it?
   b. How do we phase the introduction of services to maximize growth and impact and minimize our initial set-up costs?
   c. Are there different ways of realizing our capabilities – through partnering, buying an existing firm with those capabilities or working with an adviser who has delivered these successfully in the past?

DISCOVERY QUESTION 3:
HOW DO WE CREATE ADAPTIVE LIVING STRUCTURES AND ENVIRONMENTS IN WHICH PEOPLE THRIVE?

Hopefully, if we can answer the two earlier questions, then we will have the essence of a great organization – purpose and the capabilities to realize that purpose. However, we need to create dynamic and living structures that do the following:

- Enable people to understand their role within well-defined teams, groups and functions – like healthy cells in the body.
- Develop ways to coordinate action across the organization through clarity of decision-making and governance – like the body coordinates its systems (muscular, nervous, cardiovascular, digestive etc.).

To address these two elements, this book introduced two concepts that you can test in your own organization: whole work teams and coordinating systems.

WHOLE WORK TEAMS: HOW CAN WE CREATE 'SELF-IMPROVING CELLS' IN OUR ORGANIZATIONS?

Living organizations are built around groups that have a clear purpose and the autonomy to plan, do and improve their performance in delivering this purpose. I call these groups 'whole work teams' and this book has given examples of specific forms of such teams, including kaizen teams, agile development squads and quality circles (see *Table 6*). Whatever the specific structure you choose, good questions to ask about the groups you build are:

1. What is the purpose and significant output of the group? How would you measure it?
2. What people (skills and roles) do you need in the group to achieve the purpose?
3. What development and tools do the group need to help them innovate and improve?
4. How can the team leader and organization ensure the conditions for continuous improvement?

HOW CAN WE ENSURE COORDINATION AND BALANCE IN ORGANIZATIONAL STRUCTURE?

While cells in the body are able to regulate and sustain themselves, they need to coordinate with other parts of the body in sub-systems to perform important tasks (such as walking and digestion). Organizations need to link together around these core processes and sub-systems. *Chapter 7* introduced the concept of a value chain as the basis of 'clusters of cells' that come together to deliver important stages of work relating to client and customer needs. *Figure 13* gave the example of a scientific services company, showing how it formed an account team and a service delivery team to deliver against the various stages of its customers' requirements.

In a living organization, it is important to identify the various teams that come together to deliver on customer requirements. Each team should be a 'whole work team,' as related in the previous section. This ensures employee engagement and the capacity to grow personally and improve as a team. In working out how you should cluster teams together consider the following questions:

- What is the overall purpose of this part of the organization (e.g. sales and service management)?
- What are the key steps in this process of delivering on purpose?
- How can you break the process down into 'whole work' steps so teams can plan, do and improve their work (e.g. a sales team could look at customer satisfaction and sales growth, and a delivery team could look at reliability and time to deliver)?
- How can you ensure effective coordination and communication across these steps (e.g. through an overall sales and service leader, e-coordination and aligned measures)?

DISCOVERY QUESTION 4:
CAN WE RECOGNIZE WHEN WE NEED TO EMBRACE THE NEXT MAJOR STAGE OF DEVELOPMENT?

By this question, the goal is to have reached a point where we feel our organization has got the basics in place. We have a clarity of purpose, are clear on what we need to be good at, and have organizational processes, structures and governance that can release people's potential. However, organizations, like people, reach times when they need to 'grow up' into a new life stage, in the way that a teenager might when they leave home to start a new job. My research suggests there are at least five stages of growth, as characterized back in *Figure 24*. At each stage of development, there looms a point of crisis where an organization needs to shift its way of operating to address the issues that growth creates. These are 'good problems' but they need to be recognized as a signal to shift significant aspects of the organization, such as team and organizational structures, leadership approach, employee empowerment and how activity is coordinated.

As you and your leadership become aware of these issues arising, some useful questions to ask are:

- What image or analogy would you use for the stage of growth that the organization is in (e.g. 'start-up toddler,' 'awkward teenager' or 'learned elder')?
- Is the organizing growing successfully? What is working well?
- Are there signs of crisis or underlying issues?
- What phase of development are you at (refer back to *Figure 24*)?

- What is the nature of the challenge or crisis the organization is facing?
- What action should you (or the leadership) consider as a result to successfully move the organization into the next stage of growth?

DISCOVERY QUESTION 5:
HOW DO WE EMBRACE WIDER RELATIONSHIPS AND PARTNERSHIPS TO REMAIN DYNAMIC AND RELEVANT TO THE FUTURE?

Like the previous question, this question builds on success in tackling earlier challenges. As described in the stages of growth framework (see *Figure 24*), organizations need to adapt to their size and circumstances as they grow and develop. Larger organizations run into issues with coordination and agility, slowing their progress. Bain & Company's growth paradox analysis of large companies reveals that only about 12% manage to maintain consistent growth after reaching maturity.[91] According to this growth paradox, larger firms diversify away from their core strengths, leading to challenges in sustaining customer focus and growth.

This last question aims to combat this tendency, considering how a living organization embraces its environment, ensuring agility and 'zero distance' from the customer while leveraging wider partnerships and relationships to continue to grow. *Chapter 10* introduced the concepts of collaborative, networked and ecosystem organizations, which can help firms embrace the benefits of scale with the beauty of micro-enterprises.

If yours is a larger or more mature organization, consider the following questions around how you might embrace the benefits of this way of organizing away from larger, bureaucratic structures.

Firstly, consider: **what type of structure does your organization currently have** on a scale from bureaucratic command (1) to network (10)?

Secondly, think about **how to enable more of a network structure for your organization** based on the characteristics identified in *Chapter 10*:

- **Team-based empowerment:**
    › What would be a logical team structure to base your organization around? An example is a customer-focused team but note that you will likely need a mix of team types.
    › Are these 'whole work teams' (see *Chapter 6*) that have: a clear purpose; a plan, do and improve cycle; and outcome-based measures?
- **Enablement** – do the teams have the following areas identified in *Chapter 10*?
    › Entrepreneurial mindset.
    › Empowering leadership.
    › Shared purpose.
- **Ability to adapt** – does the team have the ability to adapt in the following ways?
    › Respond to changing customer needs (while being close enough to the customer to do this).
    › Control budgets and the team's own profitability as appropriate to the work.
    › Reward, motivate and attract appropriate staff and skills.
- **Customer-driven incentives:**
    › Are there organization-wide and team-based reward mechanisms that are aligned around sustainable, long-term customer satisfaction?
    › Are the KPIs (key performance indicators) at team level in line with broader organizational aims?

WHERE NOW?

An organization's ability to learn, and translate that learning into action rapidly, is the ultimate competitive advantage.[92]

Jack Welch,
former CEO of General Electric

The glory of God is man fully alive.

Paraphrased from Saint Irenaeus,
2nd-century bishop

You may believe that living organizations are the future for business reasons, for human and moral reasons, or (like me) both. Modern workplaces still waste a huge amount of human talent in archaic, bureaucratic command-and-control structures. Hopefully you have seen evidence in the stories and approaches shared in this book that better is possible, indeed essential. So, where might this journey to better take us and how can you take your next steps on this journey?

A good place to start is your own team, firm, charity or community organization – thinking about now and the future:

- What is it like today? What are the frustrations and fruit of the organization today?
- Think five years ahead. What is your aspiration for the organization? What would people be working on, speaking about and collaborating on together? What would be different from today?
- What does being a 'human-centred, living organization' mean to you in your context?

What ideas and resources might you draw on from this book?

- If you want to take a **thorough, systematic approach** then consider working through the five discovery questions in *Chapter 13* (which link back to the seven living organization characteristics in *Table 2*).
- If you are aware of particular issues in your organization and would prefer to act as an **organizational doctor**, then use the organizational illness and health framework introduced in *Figure 29*.
- If you want to **address specific issues in your own organization**, you may find it helpful to look at the key points summaries and application exercises at the end of each chapter. For instance, *Chapter 8* offers a variety of insights into how to develop individual, team and organization learning and embrace a growth mindset.

Beyond this, there are many other useful resources and sources of further help, including:

- **Living Work Consulting** (www.livingworkconsulting.com) – This website features the approaches and models that my team and I use as part of our consulting approach. You can also contact me through the website with any questions.
- **EODF (European Organization Design Forum)** (https://eodf.eu) – This is a Europe-wide practitioner base that I co-founded to bring together the best and latest thinking in the design and development of future organizations.
- **Henley Business School's People & Organizational Change programmes** (https://www.henley.ac.uk/corporate-development/open-programmes) – Henley Business School offers short executive education programmes, particularly under the "People & Organizational Change" banner (filter on this page).

Finally, good luck on the journey. We are on the frontier of new types of organization that release the human spirit and enable human flourishing. Join the vanguard of this movement!

REFERENCES

1. "AP, Automotive Products or Lockheed Brakes" (Leamington History Group), last modified 23 May 2016, https://leamingtonhistory.co.uk/ap-automotive-products-or-lockheed-brakes.

2. "Case Studies: Nissan (NMUK)" (Invest North East England), accessed 20 November 2024, https://investnortheastengland.co.uk/case-studies/nissan.

3. Ibid.

4. Further explanation can be found at "What are Industry 4.0, the Fourth Industrial Revolution, and 4IR?" (McKinsey & Company), last modified 17 August 2022, https://www.mckinsey.com/featured-insights/mckinsey-explainers/what-are-industry-4-0-the-fourth-industrial-revolution-and-4ir.

5. *State of the Contact Centre 2023: Activating the Agent of the Future* (Calabrio, 2023), accessed 20 November 2024, https://www.callcentrehelper.com/images/resources/2023/calabrio-state-of-contact-center-report-20230927.pdf.

6. *2021 Talkdesk Global Contact Center KPI Benchmarking Report* (Talkdesk, 2021), accessed 20 November 2024, https://infra-cloudfront-talkdeskcom.svc.talkdeskapp.com/talkdesk_com/2021-Talkdesk-global-contact-center-KPI-benchmarking-report-sl_swap.pdf.

7. State of the Global Workplace, Gallup 2024, accessed 27th Dec 2024, https://www.gallup.com/workplace/349484/state-of-the-global-workplace.aspx.

8. Based on "Employee Engagement: Where Does Your Country Rank?" (Korn Ferry), accessed 20 November 2024, https://www.kornferry.com/insights/briefings-magazine/issue-27/employee-engagement; *Are You Missing Something? Engaging and Enabling Employees for Success* (HayGroup, 2020), accessed 20 November 2024, https://wp.workplaceinnovation.org/wp-content/uploads/sites/2/2020/08/hay_group_engaging_and_enabling_employees_for_succes.pdf.

9. "About Us" (Buurtzorg), accessed 20 November 2024, https://www.buurtzorg.com/about-us.

10. Quoted in *ibid*.

11. "The Buurtzorg Model" (Buurtzorg), accessed 20 November 2024, https://www.buurtzorg.com/about-us/buurtzorgmodel.

12. "Our Organization" (Buurtzorg), accessed 20 November 2024, https://www.buurtzorg.com/about-us/our-organization.

References

13. "Buurtzorg's Model of Care" (Buurtzorg), accessed 20 November 2024, https://www.buurtzorg.com/about-us/buurtzorgmodel.

14. Ibid.

15. Ibid.

16. Ibid.

17. Michael Schuman, "Zhang Ruimin's Haier Power" (Haier), last modified 22 April 2014, https://www.haier.com/global/press-events/news/20140426_142723.shtml.

18. Ibid.

19. Ibid.

20. "Our Culture" (Haier Europe), accessed 20 November 2024, https://corporate.haier-europe.com/en-gb/about-us/our-culture.

21. Average company lifespan on Standard & Poor's 500 Index, accessed 27th December 2024, https://www.statista.com/statistics/1259275/average-company-lifespan/#

22. The seven characteristics of life are summarized at both "The 7 Unmistakable Characteristics of Life" (BiologyWise), accessed 20 November 2024, https://biologywise.com/characteristics-of-life, and "The Characteristics of Life" (SUNY ER Services), accessed 20 November 2024, https://courses.lumenlearning.com/suny-wmopen-biology1/chapter/the-characteristics-of-life.

23. "Buurtzorg's Model of Care" (Buurtzorg), accessed 20 November 2024, https://www.buurtzorg.com/about-us/buurtzorgmodel.

24. "Development History" (Haier Europe), accessed 20 November 2024, https://corporate.haier-europe.com/en-gb/about-us/history.

25. "Siemens Strengthens Core Activities" (Siemens), last modified 28 November 2012, https://press.siemens.com/global/en/pressrelease/siemens-strengthens-core-activities-acquisition-invensys-rail-divestment-baggage.

26. Google: https://about.google/; Apple: https://www.apple.com/about/; Microsoft: https://www.microsoft.com/en-us/about; Amazon: https://www.aboutamazon.com/; Meta (Facebook): https://about.meta.com/; Tesla: https://www.tesla.com/about; Netflix: https://jobs.netflix.com/values; Nike: https://purpose.nike.com/; Coca-Cola: https://www.coca-colacompany.com/company/purpose; Disney: https://thewaltdisneycompany.com/; IKEA: https://about.ikea.com/; Unilever: https://www.unilever.com/planet-and-society/. All accessed on 2nd January 2025.

27. Jim Collins and Jerry I. Porras, *Built to Last: Successful Habits of Visionary Companies* (London: Random House, 2005).

28. Arie de Geus, *The Living Company: Growth, Learning and Longevity in Business* (London: Nicholas Brealey Publishing, 1999).

29. The 4Ps of marketing are price, promotion, place and product.

30. Looking Back on the Brilliant, Complex, and Often Difficult Leadership Style of Steve Jobs, accessed 2nd Jan 2025, https://harver.com/blog/looking-back-on-the-brilliant-complex-and-often-difficult-leadership-of-steve-jobs/

31. See Patrick Lencioni, *The Five Dysfunctions of a Team* (San Francisco: Jossey-Bass 2002) and Ruth Wageman, Debra A. Nunes, James A. Burruss and J. Richard Hackmann, *Senior Leadership Teams: What It Takes to Make Them Great* (Boston: Harvard Business School Press, 2008).

32. World Café Facilitation Method, accessed 2nd January 2025, https://theworldcafe.com/key-concepts-resources/world-cafe-method/

33. Ederson is known by this single name.

34. Useful sources on this topic include George Stalk, Jr, Philip Evans and Lawrence E. Shulman, "Competing on Capabilities: The New Rules of Corporate Strategy" (*Harvard Business Review*), last modified March–April 1992, https://hbr.org/1992/03/competing-on-capabilities-the-new-rules-of-corporate-strategy; Norm Smallwood and Dave Ulrich, "Capitalizing on Capabilities" (*Harvard Business Review*), last modified June 2004, https://hbr.org/2004/06/capitalizing-on-capabilities.

35. Key capabilities of Amazon adapted from source information, accessed on 2nd January 2025, https://www.aboutamazon.eu/who-we-are

36. "Business Current Account" (Starling Bank), accessed 21 June 2024, https://www.starlingbank.com/business-account.

37. Adapted from "Talking Tech: Starling Bank" (BDO), accessed 20 November 2024, https://www.bdo.co.uk/en-gb/insights/industries/technology-media-and-life-sciences/talking-tech-starling-bank; "Beyond Change: Side by Side with Starling Bank to Reinvent Banking" (PwC), accessed 20 November 2024, https://www.pwc.co.uk/issues/transformation/case-studies-and-insights/starling-bank.html;

38. Adapted from Beth Stackpole, "Overdue: A New Organizing Model for IT" (MIT Sloan), last modified 8 November 2019, https://mitsloan.mit.edu/ideas-made-to-matter/overdue-a-new-organizing-model-it.

39. Source information from websites, accessed 2nd January 2025, Operational Excellence at Nissan Sunderland, https://www.stratagia.co.uk/post/operational-excellence-in-action-at-nissan-sunderland; Nissan's AI Integration in Design and Production, https://www.carexpert.com.au/car-news/nissan-uses-ai-and-machine-learning-for-design-and-production; Nissan's Next-Gen Factory Technology, https://www.automotivemanufacturingsolutions.com/nissan/nissan-lines-up-its-next-gen-factory-

References

technology/39876.article; Nissan's Adoption of Predictive Simulation, https://www.automotivepurchasingandsupplychain.com/digital-twins-nissan-adopts-predictive-simulation-in-sunderland-uk-plant/; Nissan's Manufacturing Hub in Sunderland, https://careersatnissan.co.uk/life-at-nissan/manufacturing-hub/

40. The Effect of Team Size on the Performance of Continuous Improvement Teams: Is Seven Really the Magic Number?, Daryl Powell, Rafael Lorenz, HAL Open Science, https://inria.hal.science/hal-02419219/document

41. Toyota's Kaizen approach increased steel yield by 12.7% over seven years, accessed 2nd January 2025, https://gearshifters.org/toyota/how-toyota-uses-kaizen/

42. GE's Six Sigma implementation saved nearly $700M by 1997 and $2.5B by 2000, accessed 2nd January 2025, https://6sigma.com/case-study-general-electric-six-sigma/

43. Spotify's Agile methodology ensures fast feedback adaptation and continuous user experience improvement, accessed 2nd January 2025, https://www.agileconnection.com/article/success-agile-spotify

44. Tata Steel's Quality Circles reduced energy use, cutting costs and environmental impact significantly, accessed 2nd January 2025, https://www.tatasteel.com/media/

45. Thoughts on failure modes of Kaizen, accessed 2nd January 2025, https://theleanthinker.com/2019/06/12/thoughts-on-failure-modes-of-kaizen-events/

46. The Effect of Team Size on the Performance of Continuous Improvement Teams: Is Seven Really the Magic Number?, Daryl Powell, Rafael Lorenz, HAL Open Science, https://inria.hal.science/hal-02419219/document

47. Toyota's Kaizen approach increased steel yield by 12.7% over seven years, accessed 2nd January 2025, https://gearshifters.org/toyota/how-toyota-uses-kaizen/

48. GE's Six Sigma implementation saved nearly $700M by 1997 and $2.5B by 2000, accessed 2nd January 2025, https://6sigma.com/case-study-general-electric-six-sigma/

49. Ibid.

50. Spotify's Agile methodology ensures fast feedback adaptation and continuous user experience improvement, accessed 2nd January 2025, https://www.agileconnection.com/article/success-agile-spotify

51. Ibid.

52. "Buurtzorg Web" (Buurtzorg), accessed 20 November 2024, https://www.buurtzorg.com/innovation/buurtzorg-web/ and https://www.aneo.eu/en/blog/networked-self-management-buurtzorg

53. Elliott Jaques, Requisite organization: A Total System for Effective Managerial Organization and Managerial Leadership for the 21st Century, 2nd ed. (Arlington: Cason Hall, 1998).

54. "Our Vision" (ChildFund), accessed 20 November 2024, https://www.childfund.org/about-us.

55. Ibid.

56. "Where We Work" (ChildFund), accessed 20 November 2024, https://www.childfund.org/about-us/our-approach/where-we-work.

57. Paul Lambert and Simon Thane, "The Missing Middle: Strategic Alignment and Empowerment," *People and Strategy Magazine* 34, no. 4 (2012): p52-55.

58. See Carol S. Dweck, *The New Psychology of Success* (London: Random House, 2007).

59. Adapted from ibid.

60. David Orenstein, "MIT Scientists Discover Fundamental Rule of Brain Plasticity" (MIT News), last modified 22 June 2018, https://news.mit.edu/2018/mit-scientists-discover-fundamental-rule-of-brain-plasticity-0622#.

61. Robert J. Doman, "Sensory Deprivation" (NACD), accessed 20 November 2024, https://www.nacd.org/sensory-deprivation.

62. David A. Kolb, *Experiential Learning: Experience as the Source of Learning and Development*, Vol. 1 (Englewood Cliffs, NJ: Prentice-Hall, 1984).

63. Ikujiro Nonaka and Hirotaka Takeuchi, *The Knowledge-Creating Company: How Japanese Companies Create the Dynamics of Innovation* (Oxford: Oxford University Press, 1991).

64. Paul Lambert, "Development of the People Capability of Applications Management Professionals in a Federal Organization" (MSc thesis, Sheffield Hallam University, 2006).

65. Larry E. Greiner, "Evolution and Revolution as Organizations Grow" (*Harvard Business Review*), last modified May–June 1998, https://hbr.org/1998/05/evolution-and-revolution-as-organizations-grow.

66. Size of audit and accounting service market from research sites, accessed 2nd January 2025, https://www.mordorintelligence.com/industry-reports/europe-auditing-services-market and https://www.ibisworld.com/europe/industry/accounting-auditing/200284/

67. The discussion of FAVI in this section builds on two articles written by Corporate Rebels, accessed 2nd January 2025, https://www.corporate-rebels.com/blog/zobrist and https://www.corporate-rebels.com/blog/favi-part-2

68. Joost Minnaar, "FAVI: How Zobrist Broke Down FAVI's Command-and-Control Structures" (Corporate Rebels), last modified 4 January 2017, https://www.corporate-rebels.com/blog/zobrist.

69. Ibid.

70. The Atelier Philosophy of Rolls-Royce 'Bespoke', accessed 2nd January 2025, https://www.motorbiscuit.com/atelier-philosophy-rolls-royce-bespoke/

71. Ashby, W. Ross. An Introduction to Cybernetics. London: Chapman & Hall, 1956, Chapter 11, titled "Requisite Variety." Page 202-218.

72. Martin Reeves, Chairman of the BCG Henderson Institute, in his article "Think Biologically: Messy Management for a Complex World," published by the Boston Consulting Group in 2017, accessed 2nd Jan 2025, https://www.bcg.com/publications/2017/think-biologically-messy-management-for-complex-world

73. Hsieh, T. (2010). Delivering Happiness: A Path to Profits, Passion, and Purpose. Business Plus

74. Brian J. Robertson, *Holacracy: The New Management System for a Rapidly Changing World* (London: Penguin, 2016).

75. Alex Hirst and Lizzie Penny, *WorkStyle* (London: John Murray, 2022).

76. The information on ASA Group is drawn from the synthesis of an interview with Emanuele Quintarelli at "Manufacturing as an Ecosystem of Entrepreneurial Innovation at ASA Group" (Boundaryless), last modified 7 February 2024, https://boundaryless.io/blog/manufacturing-ecosystem-innovation-at-asa.

77. Haier was introduced in Chapter 2 and has developed more detailed rules and insights on how to develop and shape an ecosystemic organization model.

78. Draws on David Plouffe, The Audacity to Win: The Inside Story and Lessons of Barack Obama's Historic Victory (New York: Viking, 2009).

79. McKinsey & Company. "Changing Change Management." McKinsey & Company, July 2015. Accessed January 2, 2025. https://www.mckinsey.com/featured-insights/leadership/changing-change-management.

80. Gartner. "Changing Change Management." Gartner, accessed January 2, 2025. https://www.gartner.com/en/human-resources/trends/changing-change-management.

81. Prosci. "12 Change Management Principles and Best Practices." Prosci, September 2024. Accessed January 2, 2025. https://www.prosci.com/blog/change-management-principles.

82. Drink driving analysis and statistics come from two main sources, accessed 2nd Jan 2025: GOV.UK. "Reported Road Casualties in Great Britain Involving Illegal Alcohol Levels: 2021." Last modified February 28, 2023. https://www.gov.uk/government/statistics/reported-road-casualties-in-great-britain-involving-illegal-alcohol-levels-2021. Statista. "Number of Accidents Caused by Drink-Driving in Great Britain (UK) from 1979 to 2020." Accessed January 2, 2025. https://www.statista.com/statistics/323129/accidents-caused-by-drink-driving-in-great-britain-uk-time/.

83. Imai, Masaaki. Kaizen: The Key to Japan's Competitive Success. New York: McGraw-Hill, 1986

84. © Living Work Consulting Ltd (2024).

85. "About Us" (Lego), accessed 20 November 2024, https://www.lego.com/en-gb/aboutus.

86. Generally, in the UK, people over 65 years of age are considered elderly.

87. The information on Intrepid Travel is drawn from: Intrepid Travel. "Our Purpose." Accessed January 2, 2025. https://www.intrepidtravel.com/us/purpose and Intrepid Travel. "How It All Began: The History of Intrepid Travel." Accessed January 2, 2025. https://www.intrepidtravel.com/en/about/how-it-began.

88. Victor Frankl, *Man's Search for Meaning* (Boston: Beacon Press, 1959).

89. Jim Collins and Jerry I. Porras, *Built to Last: Successful Habits of Visionary Companies* (London: Random House, 2005).

90. Chris Zook and James Allen, *The Founder's Mentality: How to Overcome the Predictable Crises of Growth* (Boston: Harvard Business Review Press, 2016).

91. Welch, Jack. Jack: Straight from the Gut. New York: Warner Books, 2001.

ACKNOWLEDGEMENTS

I have loved writing my first book. It's been an opportunity to bring together many years of working with great clients, colleagues, academics and many other friends. The book reflects experiences from family, community, charities, public sector bodies and the world of commerce. So, I have a broad group of people to thank for helping in the formation and writing of it.

I start with the "**home team**," led by my beautiful and capable wife, Juliette, for her love, reflections and encouragement. To my daughters, Hannah and Jenny, for our stimulating conversations about life, education and work around the dinner table. There is the "wider family team" that includes my dad (an excellent reviewer, even at 90!), my ever-loving mum, my sister, Tina, and my brother-in-law, Hugh. My parents cultivated a home atmosphere in which we were encouraged to think for ourselves to get at the truth and be our best – thank you!

Then there's been a "**publishing team**" who helped me to understand how to write engaging and practical material. This has included the fabulous team at LID Publishing of Martin Liu, Alec Egan, Aiyana Curtis (my editor), Caroline Li (design) and Teya Ucherdzhieva. Particular thanks to Aiyana for not just reviewing but providing great suggestions for improvement, and Alec for his encouragement around style and engaging stories.

On my writing journey, I've journeyed with ex-colleagues who I see as my "**writing inspiration team**" and gave me great steers. Firstly, Steven d'Souza, who I met at Korn Ferry when he had already written five books, including *Not Knowing*, co-authored with Diana Renner, that won the Chartered Management Institute's 'Management Book of the Year' award in the UK. He was generous with his time and contacts and set me off on this journey. Then there is Professor Mary Cianni, also from Korn Ferry, now at New York University, and author of *The Consultant's Compass*. Mary and I have spoken regularly over the past year, testing one another's thinking and ideas. Lastly, my former Prophet Partner colleague, Michael Lopez, and author of *Change: Six science-backed strategies to transform your brain, body, and behaviour*, has been a great inspiration. Michael is able to encourage, challenge and shape all within the same sentence!

One of the great joys of consulting for over 25 years is that *many of my clients have become great friends*. You will see many of the names of the "**client team**" in the testimonials. The work we did together is the central thread of this book, so I will pick out some highlights here. I am deeply grateful to Phil Evans, Director General of Eumetsat (Climate Focussed Satellite Agency), who I worked with to both shape the leadership and organization of two firms he has led. Our intellectual sparring and dinner conversations have sharpened my practice. Nick Elliott, CEO at two large defence firms, is another provocateur who doesn't just accept the "easy answer," and has allowed me to help him and others shape innovative, future focused organizations. Simon Betty, who leads a European healthcare organization, has allowed me to be a true "trusted advisor," as well as friend, as he's led and shaped major real estate firms. He also educated me on the best restaurants in Berlin! There are many others – Kini Pathmanathan (Smiths Industries Director), Alexandra Bode-Tunje (Change Grow Live), Lt Gen Paul Jaques (Defence Equipment), Tim Rowntree (Defence Equipment), Colin Brown (Crossrail), Peter Cheese (Chartered Institute of Personnel and Development), Dhanmita Boodhna (Hertfordshire Police), Dawn Brodrick OB (NHS and DWP), Ian Cope (Office of National Statistics), Jason Wenham (Network Rail), and many others I undoubtedly should have mentioned. It's been a pleasure to work as true partners, learning from one another.

Another joy is when *friends become clients and fellow advisors*. I call this group the "**friends team**." They include Steve Craggs (Baker McKenzie), Giles Mahoney (NHS), John Lee (FIT Remuneration),

Richard Deakin (NATS and Stratospheric Solutions), Stephen Graham (Hexagon Manufacturing Intelligence), Ian Causebrook (Tear Fund), Piers Hollier (Brambles), Phil Rice (PA Consulting), and many others. It's always a pleasure when a "pint down the pub" turns into an opportunity to solve organizational problems together and make a difference.

There was also the "**shapers team**," who helped refine ideas and concepts before they made it into the book. My former colleagues from Tricordant Consultants helped me to understand the human shape of work many years ago. A particular shout out to Alastair Mitchell-Baker, Roger Greene, Nick Richmond and Simon Thane. Thank you for letting me build on these ideas. I am also gratefully to Mark Greene, David Leeds and David Walker from LICC (London Institute of Contemporary Christianity) who refined the ideas about the different aspects of humans (identity, physical, cognitive and emotional) and how these related to organization. Alex Hirst and Ed Horrocks, from the Hoxby Collective, provided brilliant insights into new ways of working based on "WorkStyle" (Alex's book). Emmanuelle Quintarelli, director of Boundaryless, provided deep insights into ecosystemic organizations – the best of which were shared over a very tasty dinner in Milan! Professor Nick Kemsley, my former Korn Ferry colleague and Director of the HR and OC Centre at Henley Business School, has been a confidant for many years and we've shaped each other's thinking around people and organizations. Thank you, Nick.

Finally, I come to the "**mentors team**" – people who have been with me on the journey of life and work for a long time. Paul Valler, former Finance and Ops Director at Hewlett Packard, helped to shape my work, thinking and life over a decade in regular mentoring sessions. Paul combines sharp thinking, deep character and a ready wit. Janet Windeatt, my former colleague from PA Consulting, has been, with her husband Terry, a friend for a couple of decades. She has provided inspiration and feedback on the book, alongside applying these ideas in practice together as consultants. Chris Blakeley leads the Waverley Community and, until recently, Waverley Consulting. He is the epitome of a deeply reflective practitioner who leads from the heart in addressing the emotional, behavioural and attitudinal issues blocking the growth of people and organizations. You continue to be an inspiration, Chris!

Finally, and certainly most important of all, I give all thanks to God, the Father, the Son, and the Holy Spirit for all that I am.

ABOUT THE AUTHOR

Paul Lambert is the founding director of Living Work Consulting and programme director of the People & Organizational Change executive masterclasses at Henley Business School (a world top 20 executive education provider). He works with clients to deliver innovative, human-centric solutions to real-world people and organizational challenges.

Paul has worked for over 25 years helping senior teams lead effectively, design client-centric operating models, develop the future workforce and create high-performance cultures across a range of market sectors. His past work includes the redesign of a large European digital real estate firm, a two-year transformation programme for a UK defence equipment agency with 12,500 staff, and the workforce planning for two multi-billion-pound rail programmes for Network Rail in the UK.

Paul is a founder of the EODF (European Organization Design Forum), which connects leading organization design practitioners across Europe and the USA. He previously led the workforce transformation and organizational development services of Korn Ferry, PA Consulting and Prophet Consulting. He speaks regularly at HR and business conferences and writes for both the specialist and mainstream press on workforce and organizational issues.

BOOK SUMMARY

Our world is a rich and dynamic environment in which life moves through seasons and evolves over time. Our political, social and economic life is permeated with major trends and movements affecting our lives and cultures. However, in organizations, this level of external disruption has been addressed through relatively conventional and static ways of organizing.

This original book offers an alternative to this stalemate through a fundamental shift in mindset. Organizations, like people, need to be seen as living, evolving organisms – there is no single way to structure and lead a company. This book is based on a living model of organizations with a clear purpose expressed through physical, emotional and cognitive characteristics – reflecting the people within them.

Written by international consulting director and business school lecturer Paul Lambert, this book includes powerful and detailed examples throughout. These include Nissan, Apple, Haier, Buurtzorg, the Hoxby Collective, ChildFund, FAVI, Barack Obama's campaign organization, a global oil and gas firm, and an international accountancy firm. Application exercises and summaries of the key points in each chapter allow the reader to immediately apply the insights to their own organization.